MOU_____E
GUIDE

West Midlands

by
Dave Taylor

THE ERNEST PRESS

Published by The Ernest Press 2000
© Dave Taylor 2000

ISBN 0 948153 61 X
A CIP record for this book is available from
The British Library, Wetherby

Typeset from the author's disk by Stanningley Serif
Printed by Colorcraft

Disclaimer:
Whilst we have made every effort to achieve accuracy in the production of
material for use in this guide, the author and publisher cannot take
responsibility for trespass, irresponsible riding, any loss or damage to
persons or property suffered as a result of the route descriptions or
advice offered in this book.
The inclusion of a route in this guide does not guarantee that the track will
remain a right of way. If conflict with a landowner occurs, please be polite
and leave by the shortest possible route, then check the access situation
with the relevant authority.
It is worthwhile emphasising that riders should give way to both horse
riders and pedestrians, and should make every effort to warn others of
their approach.

CONTENTS

SHROPSHIRE

ACKNOWLEDGEMENTS

This guide would not have been completed without the help and support of my wife, Carol. Without her patience and encouragement I would not have been able to continue, particularly on those days when the weather seemed determined to frustrate all attempts at mountain biking. My wife has helped in many ways, from researching routes to proof reading manuscripts, as well as consoling me at the end of a hard day!

Thanks must also go to my son Alex for inspiring me to continue. His growing interest in biking and fresh enthusiasm to help with some of the routes, particularly in Cannock Chase, have also provided me with the energy needed to complete the book.

I would also like to thank all those helpful people at the various county councils whom I have pestered on occasions in my efforts to ensure that the routes contained within this book are legal. In particular, I would like to thank Shona Lewis, Rights of Way Officer for Shropshire County Council, who has received a continual stream of enquiries about rights of way, and who has always managed to reply so swiftly.

My thanks also go to Mr Beeston of Lower Wood Corner Farm near Ashley Heath for allowing a short section of track to be used as an extension of the dead-end bridleway in Bishop's Wood. Please respect this generosity and always give way to other users, be they on foot or horse.

Lastly, thanks to all those mountain bikers I met whilst out doing these routes. Their friendliness and enthusiasm also helped provide me with the inspiration to complete this guide.

The West Midlands

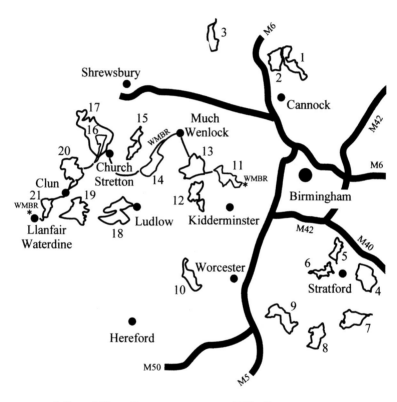

1 Cannock Chase - East
2 Cannock Chase - West
3 Ashley Heath
4 Wellesbourne
5 Henley-in-Arden
6 Alcester
7 Chipping Campden & Hidcote
8 Broadway
9 Bredon and Dumbleton
10 Suckley Hills
11 Kinver, and beyond!
12 Wyre Forest
13 Severn Valley
14 Wenlock Edge
15 Hope Bowdler
16 Long Mynd - the quiet way
17 Long Mynd and the Stiperstones
18 Ludlow
19 Hopton Castle
20 Clun & Bury Ditches
21 Clun & Offa's Dyke
22 West Midlands Bike Route

PREFACE

Since producing the previous version of this book, *Mountain Bike Guide: The Midlands* (The Ernest Press 1994), it became clear that many alterations needed to be made in the re-write. In making these changes I have endeavoured in various ways to produce an even better guide.

Firstly, the original guide covered a very wide area, perhaps too wide. However, it became clear in my researching that there were many more routes out there waiting to be discovered. As a consequence, I decided to split the book into two parts. The first book, *Mountain Bike Guide: East Midlands*, was published by The Ernest Press in 1998. This, the second book, covers the West Midlands including the counties of Staffordshire, Shropshire, Hereford and Worcestershire, and also the western half of Warwickshire and a little bit of Gloucestershire.

Secondly, it will be apparent from the West Midlands area map that many of the routes lie close to each other and therefore the possibility of linking them together exists. This is not a new idea. Shropshire County Council created the Jack Mytton Way, a long distance bridleway, in 1993 and I have attempted to extend and improve this route.

Thirdly, it will be clear from the original guide that my abilities at drawing maps are somewhat limited to say the least. I have attempted to rectify the problem, with the aid of new technology, and I hope that the new maps are easier to follow.

INTRODUCTION

Mountain biking and cycling is now one of the most popular participation sports in the UK, with major events such as the Malverns Classic and the Red Bull well established, and many other events organized every weekend. This sport is now no longer frowned upon as the preserve of a minority (often viewed as a nuisance), but as one that can involve all ages and abilities.

The second city of Birmingham does not immediately strike one as being the Mecca of mountain biking. True, the 'Venice of the North' does have many restored canals that can provide a pleasant Sunday morning bike ride, but this is only a limited compensation for the dedicated mountain biker. However, the countryside to the west of Birmingham rises and becomes increasingly hilly as you move towards the Welsh Border. This area has many exciting and taxing off-road possibilities. Although the West Midlands is not blessed with very many mountains there are some significant hills, and as one goes further west, the countryside has about it a more remote feel. Yet, all the routes described in this book are within an hour's drive of the centre of Birmingham.

The growth in popularity of mountain biking has seen an enormous increase in the use of bikes in areas such as the Lake District or the Dales where, unfortunately, they are sometimes perceived as yet another threat to an already over-stressed environment. Ten years ago, the only people you were likely to see in these areas were walkers and climbers. Now mountain bikes are seen as just another way to enjoy the countryside, often ridden by those who in the past might have walked. Mountain bikes add a new dimension to the thrill of the great outdoors. What can beat the buzz of a technical, rocky descent after a hard fought climb? But do we always need to go to these popular areas? This guide illustrates that there is plenty of mountain biking fun to be had in other parts of the country, which can be just as challenging in its own right.

Many owners of mountain bikes, particularly those new to the sport, do not necessarily relish the challenge of carrying a bike to the top of a 3000ft mountain, but would appreciate simple, easy to follow and reliable descriptions of where to ride off-road, legally. This book will provide some guidance for such folk, although it would be a mistake to assume that all the routes in this book are easy! In any case, given the wrong conditions even the easiest looking route can become a real challenge.

The routes described vary greatly in style and difficulty. Some would make an ideal day out for a family group, whilst the more experienced hammerhead might prefer to thrash around in an afternoon. Other routes are perhaps best savoured on a fine summers evening, when there are fewer people about and the pubs are more likely to be open. Whatever type of mountain biker you are, I am sure that you'll find that these routes will prove interesting and enjoyable. Mountain biking should not only be about having the latest bits of high-tech gear, but also about appreciating the countryside, with a little bit of fitness and a lot of fun.

ENVIRONMENT

One of my concerns as the author of this guide, has been its potential effect on the environment. Fortunately, unlike the more popular areas such as the Lake District, there is still not yet generally perceived to be a great problem with mountain bikes in the Midlands. It is hoped that, whilst it is the intention to encourage mountain biking in the area, this guide will not create problems of conflict of interest. In spite of the fact that the area contains such a large conurbation as Birmingham, the rural districts around are very quiet and often unexplored by mountain bikes. True, it would be misleading to try to suggest that it is possible to devise completely off-road routes in the area, but by linking bridleways and tracks with small country lanes it is easy to create interesting and often challenging routes.

The area is characterised by quite intensive farming and although bridleways may exist on the Ordnance Survey map, the reality can be different on the ground. The continued existence of a bridleway seems to depend to a great extent upon whether or not there is a history of horse riding in the area. Where the latter is the case, the bridleway may well have been downgraded to a footpath or lost altogether. This situation has, however, improved in recent years as many county councils struggle to record and clarify the rights of way in their area prior to the year 2000. Even where the bridleway still exists, the amount of use that it gets determines whether it is possible to ride it or not. Whatever the case, the continued use of such bridleways by mountain bikers will only be accepted by local farmers and the public if they can be persuaded that mountain bikers are essentially jolly decent country loving folk, at least in public!

Unfortunately, even with the best intentions, conflicts do arise. Since producing the original version of the guide a few problems have come to the author's notice. To illustrate this point I take the particular case of a bridleway that runs to Heathcote Farm near Wellesbourne in Warwickshire. This route was in the original Midlands guide, and because of problems appears in a modified form in this guide. The author was under the impression that the bridleway continued past the farmhouse, but this is apparently not the case. The problem would not have been so great, but for the unfortunate attitude towards the farmer from some groups of mountain bikers.

Problems can often be resolved by taking a different approach. For example, I am particularly indebted to Mr Beeston of Lower Wood Corner Farm for his permission to use a section of track (which is marked on the maps as a footpath) near Bishop's Wood. This means that, not only can mountain bikers enjoy beautiful views of the woods across the valley, they can also test their skills on a tricky little downhill section.

The author has made every attempt to ensure that the routes in this book use legal rights of way, but the existence of a route in the book is not proof that a right of way exists. If you are faced with a problem en-route, there is no point in waving the book, or a photocopy of it, at an irate farmer, who has probably lived there all his life and thinks you should not be there. Just smile nicely and leave. Check the problem out with the County Council Rights of Way people if you feel you have a just cause.

In essence, enjoy yourself in the countryside, but be considerate of others. If you follow the Off-Road and Country Codes, then you cannot go far wrong.

The Off Road Code
- Only ride where you know you have a legal right,
- Always give way to horses and pedestrians,
- Avoid animals and crops,
- Take all litter with you,
- Leave all gates as found,
- Keep the noise down,
- Don't get annoyed with anyone, it never solves problems,
- Always try to be self-sufficient, for you and your bike,
- Never create a fire hazard.

In addition to this there is of course the Country Code, issued by the Countryside Commission.

The Country Code
- Enjoy the countryside and respect its life and work,
- Guard against the risk of fire,
- Fasten all gates,
- Keep your dogs under close control,
- Keep to public rights of way across farmland,
- Use gates (and stiles) to cross fences, hedges and walls,

- Leave livestock, crops and machinery alone,
- Take your litter home,
- Help keep all water clean,
- Protect wildlife, plants and trees,
- Take special care on country roads,
- Make no unnecessary noise.

All of the above begs the question, what actually is a right of way?

RIGHTS OF WAY

The future of mountain biking is very much in the hands of those who ride mountain bikes. The whole ethos associated with mountain biking is one of fun, freedom and adventure. Although rules seem to be the antipathy of the sport, these codes need to be followed. It is very easy to be romantic about the rural landscape. In reality, particularly in the Midlands, the countryside is one big factory, albeit a very pretty one on occasions. Landowners and farmers who view the countryside as a business do not take kindly to the public, whether on foot, horse or bike, causing disruption and possibly threatening their livelihood. It is essential, therefore, to be aware of where you may ride legally.

There are four types of right of way as detailed on the OS maps, of which three are open to off-road riding.

Public Footpath – this is a right of way on foot only. Mountain bikers do not have a right of way on footpaths (unless you are given permission by the landowner). If you ride your bike onto a footpath you are committing a civil offence and as such could be sued by the landowner for damage to property. On a more practical note, footpaths will usually have a stile at each field boundary and, after trying to carry your bike over these a few times, you will begin to wonder whether it is worth it. Best advice is, keep off – no go area.

Bridleways – These are open to the public on foot, on horseback and on bicycle, provided that cyclists give way to horses and pedestrians. It is important to remember that cyclists have only had this right since 1968 and are therefore comparative newcomers, so smile nicely and give way to any walkers or horses that you see. Bridleways are usually marked by a blue waymarker, although not all local councils are as careful as they might be and, occasionally, you may only see yellow footpath markers.

BOATS – or By-ways Open to All Traffic. As the classification implies, these are open to all vehicles as well as pedestrians, horses and cyclists. Unfortunately, a minority of users of four wheel drive vehicles and motorcycles have succeeded in making a real mess of some of these excellent tracks and even the adjoining land, much to the annoyance of the landowners.

RUPPS – These are Roads Used as Public Paths. Take care with these! In the Midlands at least, these have a nasty habit of no longer existing on the ground, or have been downgraded to the status of a footpath. Where they do exist many local councils are now in the process of reclassifying these to BOATs or Bridleways.

In addition to the four types of rights of way there are also:

Unclassified County Roads – These very minor roads are often unsurfaced and are usually not maintained. Whilst not strictly 'off-road' as such, they can range in appearance from superb walled tracks, to little more than linear depressions in the ground. In effect they have the same status as a by-way but on the map it may not be clear whether they are a right of way or a private track. Consultation with the definitive map held by the Highways department of the County Council will usually clarify.

Canal towpaths – The industrial heritage of the Midlands has bequeathed an extensive network of canals and their associated towpaths. With the increase in leisure activities in general, many of these towpaths are now in excellent condition, but it is important to remember that these paths are not public rights of way. British Waterways, who own most of the canal network, do allow use of the towpaths by cyclists, subject to certain restrictions. Firstly, in order to use the path it is necessary to obtain and subsequently display a permit from British Waterways. The address is included in the appendix. Secondly, certain stretches of canal may not be available to cyclists due to, for example, the condition of the path or the towpath coinciding with a public footpath. That said, the canal system is very extensive and whilst it may not present the most challenging of off-road riding, it is often very scenic and is useful in linking more off-road sections together. Take care, however! Towpaths can be rather narrow in places and soft at the edges. Look out for low bridges and obstructions on the path. Keep your speed down and be aware, otherwise you might just take an unexpected dip in the murky waters.

Forest Tracks – A great deal of woodland is managed by Forest Enterprise on behalf of the Forestry Commission. In the past, access has been difficult, but more recently the Commission has shown a more enlightened attitude and opened up areas of their land for leisure activities, initially for walkers. All tracks on Forestry Commission land are private, unless they coincide with recognized rights of way. However, in many areas, the Commission has indicated that they are happy for bikers to use some of the gravel tracks within their forests, although this should always be checked with the local office, as restrictions may be introduced at any time. If you do use the forestry tracks, have consideration for others. There is a strong urge to 'let rip' on these tracks and as a consequence terrify the local Sunday afternoon trippers! This is a sure way to get mountain bikers banned from the forest and has already created problems in certain areas. To alleviate problems of this nature, the Forestry Commission is now making available areas specifically aimed at mountain bikers. Good examples of this are Hopton Woods, Ludow and the Wyre Forest, all of which have waymarked trails of varying difficulty. Facilities of this kind can be expected only if mountain bikers show that they are responsible users of the countryside.

EQUIPMENT

Although this guide shows that it is perfectly possible to bike off-road in the Midlands and escape the hassle of modern life, an off-road experience in Shropshire is unlikely to have the same degree of seriousness as a day out on Helvellyn. There are, however, a few points about equipment that are relevant, regardless of where you are biking.

The Bike

The type of mountain bike you prefer to ride is very much a personal choice. There is a great deal of hype surrounding mountain biking technology that, for most people, is pretty irrelevant, except when it comes to 'pose value'! Choose the best bike you can afford, but remember what you are going to put it through. A well-built rigid or hardtail may be a more sensible choice than the latest full suspension job, bedecked with numerous widgets. That said, there are a few devices that I have found particularly helpful when biking in the Midlands. As you might expect, mud can be more than a slight problem in this part of the country! Personally, I detest mudguards, but I have found the detachable Crud Catcher an excellent insurance against those unpleasant 'black outs' caused by flying mud from the front wheel when on a rapid descent. An equally useful device is the Crud Claw, which is excellent at scraping mud and bits of arable field out of the rear sprocket.

Clothing and Safety

Again, this is a very personal matter and there is more than enough advice in the magazines and books on what should be worn. In the event of a crash, however, what you are wearing could have an important effect on how well you survive! One item that is essential, is a helmet. Find one that fits well and use it! This may seem a pain at first, and helmets are not cheap, but consider the consequences of a bad crash without one. Having seen how effective they are in practice, I have no doubt about their value. Also, consider investing in a pair of gloves, they will make the ride more comfortable and protect your hands in the event of a fall. Glasses too, are a good idea. Not only do they look cool, they also keep nasties such as bugs, mud and twigs out of your eyes. Whilst on the subject of safety, it is perhaps a good idea to carry a small first-aid kit. This might include nothing more than a few plasters, a roll of bandage, lint, and a pair of scissors, but you never know when it might be needed!

Tools

Many books have been written regarding the maintenance and repair of bikes and I would not presume to improve on their advice. A basic tool kit can, however, prevent a pleasant day out from degenerating into farce. At a minimum the kit should include – a universal spanner, Allen keys, small screwdriver, tyre levers, pump, spare tube and puncture repair kit. The last three items I have found absolutely essential. A particular problem in the Midlands is the prevalence of hedges (particularly alongside canals) which, after they have been trimmed, leave nice little sharp thorns all over the track. Invest in some self-sealing inner tubes or expect puncture repairs to be the norm!

THE ROUTES

Each route is accompanied by a map, summary, details of the route, an introduction and a description. I have tried to indicate places of interest en-route within the introduction and occasionally in the description. A few words of explanation are required regarding the route details.

Grade – I have found it particularly difficult to grade these routes. A descriptive grade can only be subjective at the best of times and is always dependent on many factors. In trying to grade these routes I have assumed that the rider is of very average fitness, that is, they are neither a couch potato nor a health and fitness freak. I have also assumed that the surface conditions are reasonably good, i.e. not completely waterlogged. The ridability of some of the routes is severely affected by the surface conditions. In very wet conditions it becomes impossible to even push a bike across ploughed fields, let alone ride it. I have assumed a fairly typical (?) British summer of sunshine and showers, hence you should expect quite boggy bits in the woods. Less than ideal conditions could increase the difficulty considerably. The grades are also specific to the West Midlands. Assuming good surface conditions, many of these routes would probably be graded as easy or moderate on a national basis, if only because the hills are of modest size. This would be of little help and could be misleading, as the difficulty of these routes is frequently dependent upon the state of the ground.

I have therefore used a subjective system of grading similar to that used in rock climbing. Each grade is severely affected by personal fitness, surface conditions and should be taken with a large bucket of salt!

Easy – Few difficulties, probably uses canal tow-paths and a reasonable proportion of country lanes, only crosses fields on good tracks, little or no hill climbing.

Moderate – Some slight difficulties may be encountered, perhaps due to soft woodland tracks and occasional poor field edge bridleways. Some minor hill climbs.

Difficult – Longer duration route with more significant hill climbs. Expect some difficulties with field edge bridleways and soft woodland tracks.

Very difficult – Longer duration route with many significant hill climbs. Definitely has sections of soft woodland tracks or along field edge bridleways. Probably a more remote area and has plenty of challenges!

Time – The times can only be approximate, bearing in mind the factors described above. I have not allowed any time for cream teas, quick pints, jam butties, photos or puncture repairs!

Distance – I have tried to indicate the approximate proportion of on and off-road riding. An ideal requirement when researching the routes was that each route should be at least 50% off-road and this is mostly the case. A second requirement was that any road riding should be on as little class A or B road as possible. The vast majority of the roads used in these routes are in fact small, little used country lanes, with only the occasional use of a B road and, very occasionally, an A road.

MAPS

As will be evident from the sketch-maps for each route, I am, by no stretch of the imagination, an expert cartographer. Each map is intended only as guidance to support the route description. I would strongly recommend that the relevant Ordnance Survey map for the area be referred to for more information.

The best map to use (aside from the 1:10 000 definitive maps held by the County Councils) is the Explorer 1:25 000 series. These excellent new maps will replace the older Pathfinder series, and the detail recorded on these maps is superb and, one hopes, as up-to-date as it can be. Unfortunately, the complete list of the Explorer maps could be rather expensive, however the relevant 1:50 000 Landranger maps should prove sufficient for the purpose and you should encounter no route finding problems. The list of required maps is as follows,

Landranger
151 Stratford-upon-Avon & surrounding area
150 Worcester, The Malverns & surrounding area
149 Hereford, Leominster & surrounding area (west part of Suckley route only)
138 Kidderminster & Wyre Forest
137 Ludlow, Wenlock Edge & surrounding area
127 Stafford, Telford & surrounding area
128 Derby and Burton upon Trent (East Cannock Chase only)

Explorer
190(14) Malvern Hills and Bredon Hill
201 Knighton & Presteigne
203 Ludlow
204 Worcester & Droitwich Spa
205 Stratford-upon-Avon & Evesham
216 Welshpool & Montgomery
217 The Long Mynd & Wenlock Edge
218 Wyre Forest & Kidderminster
243 Market Drayton
244(6) Cannock Chase

KEY TO SKETCHMAP

- - - - - - - - - - -	Bridleway, usually a single track.
===========	Bridleway, BOAT, RUPP, UCR.
≈≈≈	Metalled road.
⌇	Stream or river.
🌲	Trees.
PH	Public house.
⌣	Bridge.
▮	Buildings.
†	Church.
✕	Battlefield site.
+	Deserted village.
200 △	Trig point and height in metres.
🗼	Windmill.
☼	Site of ancient fort or castle.

Cannock Chase, the Punch Bowl

East Cannock

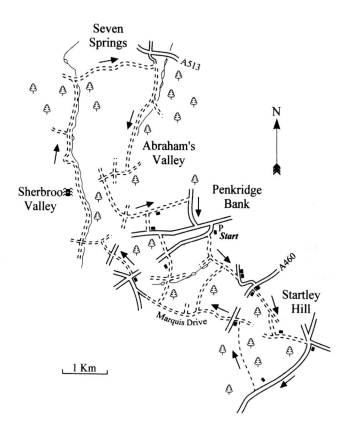

Seven Springs

A513

Abraham's Valley

N

Sherbrook Valley

Penkridge Bank

P Start

A460

Marquis Drive

Startley Hill

1 Km

Cannock Chase - East

Route Summary
Cannock Forest Centre, Miflins Valley, Startley Hill, Marquis Drive, Sherbrook Valley, Stepping Stones, Seven Springs, Abraham's Valley, Penkridge Bank, Cannock Forest Centre,

Details
Grade – Moderate
Time – 2 1/2 hrs
Distance –   24 Km
    off road – 22 Km
    on road –   2 Km
Terrain – Hills and Valleys
Surface – Good forestry tracks
Start Grid Reference – SK 018171
Maps – Explorer 6 Cannock, (Stafford and Telford L127, Derby and Burton upon Trent L128).

Introduction
Cannock Chase is a justifiably popular area with walkers, horse riders and, more recently, mountain bikers. Situated so close to the towns of Rugeley, Stafford, Cannock and the conurbation to the north of Birmingham, it forms a convenient and easily accessible area of raised heath land and forest. It is not surprising, therefore, that it is so popular. The Chase covers about 26 square miles and is designated an Area of Outstanding Natural Beauty. The forest and park contain a wealth of wild life and there are several Sites of Special Scientific Interest. In the past, there have been conflicts between mountain bikers and other users of the area, but Forest Enterprise have now set up three way-marked mountain bike routes of varying degrees of difficulty. In general, bikes are encouraged to keep to

solid tracks and bridleways only, keep the speed down, and be considerate of other users.

The Chase is well known to local mountain bikers and there are so many tracks in this beautiful area that it is difficult to recommend the 'best route'. The route suggested here takes in a large part of the Chase and uses legal bridleways almost exclusively. I would suggest that perhaps Sunday afternoon is not the best time to visit the Chase, but rather a quiet, warm summer's evening.

Route Description

The route starts at the Cannock Forest Centre. Take a left along the road for about 100m and left again along the forest road, which is also the start of one of the Forest Enterprise routes. The track soon descends and fords Stony Brook, and then after about a kilometre arrives at a lane opposite some cottages. A right turn here will bring you to the main **A460**.

Fortunately, we do not have to use the main road, but cross over to a slip road, which takes you down to the start of the track at the bottom of the Miflins valley. Go left here and up the valley, soon escaping the hassle of the road. Eventually you join up with another track, **Marquis Drive**, and continue to climb, soon arriving at a road junction. Go right and follow the road for about 1.5 km, passing the drive to the Beaudesert Golf Club. Shortly after this, you will see a track on the right, which doubles back. Follow this for a short distance until you see a notice that warns you of low flying golf balls from the left (especially if you're on a mountain bike?). Keep your hat on, your head down and scurry across the short stretch of fairway, following the bridleway! Continue straight on into the woods and follow the obvious and superb descent all the way back down to the bottom of **Marquis Drive** and then left to the main road.

Cross the road and go over the level crossing (take care!) and continue climbing up Marquis Drive. After a while the track begins to level out and eventually becomes metalled. Continue straight on until you reach the main road where you go right (straight on). Very soon you come to a crossroads. Diagonally right is a track, signed 'Heart of England Way', which leads into the woods. Follow this and at a junction do a dogleg right and then left, and continue on the bridleway. Soon you reach another junction, where you do a repeat performance. After a short distance you arrive at a road where you cross over and continue on down hill on the Heart of England Way. You arrive at a T-junction, where the route goes left and down to the **Sherbrook Valley**. Cross over the brook and go right and down a good track on the west side of the valley. Eventually you come to the Stepping Stones at the bottom of the valley, where you go right and ford Sher Brook. Follow the track, which eventually takes you round to the **Seven Springs** carpark.

Take the track, which goes roughly south-east across the clearing to the woods in the left corner. Follow the track up **Abraham's Valley** by the side of the stream and past the pools. The track climbs steadily and, ignoring any tracks to the left or right, eventually arrives at a T-junction, where you go right. After a short climb, continue straight on at the crossroads and into the woods, very soon to arrive at trig point 199m. Go left here and along a wide gravel track, which eventually bears left by the cadet huts to a crossroads of tracks. Continue straight on, going approximately east along Kingsley Wood Road, a gravel track which becomes tarmac, until you reach a lane. Go right, along Stafford Brook Road, and then left at the main road. Take the first right and back to the start of the route at the Forest Centre.

West Cannock

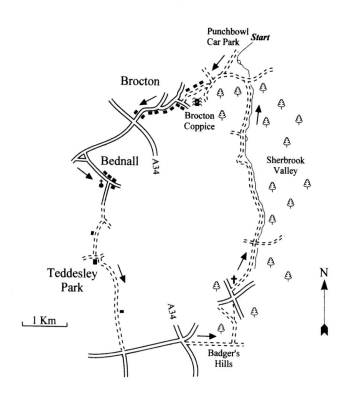

Cannock Chase - West

Route Summary
Punchbowl, Brocton Coppice, Brocton, Bednall, Teddesley Park, Badger's Hills, Broadhurst Green, Sherbrook Valley, Punchbowl.

Details
Grade – Easy
Time – 2hrs
Distance –   20km
    off road – 15km
    on road –   5km
Terrain – Some hills
Surface – Excellent forestry tracks
Start Grid Reference – SJ 984208
Maps – Explorer 6 Cannock, (Stafford, Telford & surrounding area L127)

Introduction
This nice easy route is just the thing for those new to biking, who wish to branch out and explore areas beyond the prescribed routes in forest areas. The route starts at the Punchbowl carpark and wends its way over to Brocton past the scenic "bullrush" Mere pool. At Brocton, the route leaves the Chase and makes an excursion through the pretty countryside to the west. The lanes are quiet here and the bridleway is easy going, ranging from potholed tarmac to stony farm track. After passing through the grounds of Teddesley Park, the route returns to Cannock Chase, with an excellent little hill climb up onto Badger's Hills. After passing the German Military Cemetery, a sombre reminder of the futility of war, the route takes an easy run down the Sherbrook valley and back to the start. This is not a route that is going to tax the abilities of the average

mountain biker, but it is ideal for those new to the sport, or those who need a quick fix in the short days of winter.

Those who fancy a bit more of a challenge could easily combine this route with the previous one to make a real day out. There are many possibilities in Cannock Chase and the surrounding country-side, just remember to be considerate to other users of the chase and have fun!

Route Description

Start at the **Punchbowl** carpark on the Stafford-Rugeley A513. Follow the main track into the woods, which soon brings you down to a junction of tracks on the Staffordshire Way, where you go right. Follow this to a junction of tracks by Mere Pool and continue straight on, climbing gently, until you come into the back of **Brocton** vil-lage. The pebbly track continues along the back of some smart look-ing houses on the edge of the village, eventually becoming a tarmac lane. Go right at the junction, into the village and follow the road around, until eventually you come to a crossroads on the A34. Al-though it may seem that you are leaving all the fun of the Chase behind, this little excursion into the neighbouring countryside will provide a quiet detour, with fine views. Continue straight across for Penkridge, taking care with the traffic, and along the lane. After about a kilometre you will come to a crossroads, where you go left and then straight on (left) at a T-junction for the village of **Bednall**. This quiet lane takes you into the village and, just past All Saints church and opposite an attractive half-timbered building, you will see a lane on your right with a dead-end sign.

Follow this old lane out of the village and soon it bears right and becomes a bridleway, which leads up to the main farm of **Teddesley Park**. At a T-junction go left and then right and between some farm buildings. After going through the farm the track bears left and be-comes broken and potholed. To your left you will see fine views of the Chase in the distance (don't worry, we'll soon get back there!).

Continue through the pleasant park land, past a lake and through some woods, and onto a tarmac farm road. Follow this up to a junction with a road proper, where you go left.

The road climbs gently for a little over a kilometre, back towards the Chase. At the junction with the A34, go right and then very soon you will see a lane on your left. Take this excellent bridleway, which climbs up past the young plantation of **Badger's Hills**, until you arrive at a junction of tracks. Go left here and along the bridleway which climbs a little and then starts to descend through a very quiet part of Cannock Chase. Where the main track starts to descend and bear left, you continue straight on and along a narrow single track. This eventually brings you out onto a road, where you go left to arrive at a crossroads.

Continue straight on at the crossroads and after about 100m or so you will see on your right the drive for the German Military Cemetery. Follow this drive, which is a bridleway, down past the cemetery and onto a stony track. This leads you down through the woods and into the **Sherbrook Valley**. Soon you arrive at a junction of bridleways, where you go left, then immediately right, and down the west side of the valley. This is one of the Forest Enterprise bike routes in Cannock Chase. Eventually you come to the Stepping Stones at the bottom of the valley where the FE bike route goes right, but you continue straight on along the Staffordshire Way. Soon the bridleway brings you back to the junction at the start of the route where you go right and back to the carpark.

In Cannock Chase

Gorge at Bishop's Offley

Ashley Heath

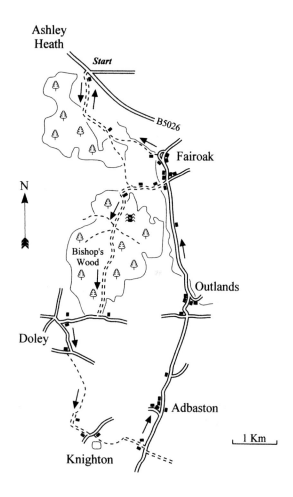

Ashley Heath

Start

B5026

Fairoak

N

Bishop's Wood

Outlands

Doley

Adbaston

1 Km

Knighton

Ashley Heath

Route Summary
Ashley Heath, Hookgate, Bishop's Wood, Doley, Knighton, Adbaston, Outlands, Fairoak, Hookgate, Ashley Heath.

Details
Grade – Easy/Mod
Time – 2 Hrs
Distance –   21km
    off road – 12km
    on road –   9km
Terrain – A bit hilly in places
Surface – Good forestry tracks with reasonable field bridleways
Start Grid Reference – SJ 748350
Maps – Stafford, Telford & surrounding area L127

Introduction
This straightforward little route explores the bridleways in the pleasant rolling countryside on the borders of Staffordshire and Shropshire near Market Drayton. The route combines some excellent forestry tracks through Bishop's Wood with some reasonable field edge bridleways between Doley and Adbaston. Although the return route is along country lanes, these are very picturesque and quiet, with a final off-road section to take you home.

Those who study the maps carefully will note that the first section of bridleway through Bishop's Wood is a dead end at SJ 756 328, but continues as a footpath to join a bridleway from Fairoak at SJ 758 325. In fact this path, which is an excellent little downhill, is well used by horse riders and other users and the author is indebted to Mr Beeston of Lower Wood Corner Farm for allowing this section to be included in the route. Please be particularly considerate to other users along this section.

Also of note is the raised area of land to the east of the hamlet of Outlands. The habitations in this area all have Offley in their name, for example, Offleyrock, Offleyhay, Offleymarsh, Offleybrook and Bishop's Offley. The latter is well worth a little detour, if only to have a pint at the pub and then take the little lane down to Offleybrook, through a very narrow and mysterious gorge.

Route Description

Start in or near Ashley Heath and follow the **B5026** south-east. Just past Hookgate you will see a bridleway on your right, which is in fact a drive to a farm. Follow this for about 1·5 km to the farm, where you go through a couple of large gates and on to a track. The farm track, which is a bridleway, bears left and goes down to the village of Fairoak, but we continue straight on into **Bishop's Wood**. The track is generally not too bad and can be mostly ridable, even after some wet weather. In fact this is one of the fun sections of the route and there are some fine views of the hills and woods here abouts. The track descends a little and comes to a clearing, where you go left. Follow along the edge of the wood, then bear right and descend steeply down a tricky, stony, but fun track (a light touch on the brakes needed here!). After going through a small bridle gate you follow along the edge of the field and on to a farm track where you continue straight on.

Follow this track across the valley and round to the left, where you will see on your right a bridleway sign and a lane, which doubles back. The track climbs steadily, bears left and arrives at a house. After going through a couple of gates (can be muddy) you follow a narrow track, which enters the next section of Bishop's Wood. Continue straight on (right-hand track) on an excellent forestry track, which descends to a junction of bridleways, where you carry straight on along a forestry gravel road. This easy 2 km section is a pleasure to ride, but all too soon the track becomes narrower and slightly boggy, and eventually brings you to a gate and out onto a country lane.

Go right at the lane and soon you reach the hamlet of **Doley**, where you go left. Follow the narrow lane along to a T-junction by a house and turn right for Soudley. After only 100m you will see a bridleway sign on your left. Follow the well-defined track along the edge of the field, through a gap and into the next field. Continue on reasonable track around the left-hand edge of the field to arrive at another gap. Go through this and follow around the right-hand edge of the field on a good farm track. Eventually this crosses a field and bears left. The track passes a farm and becomes a dirt road, which takes you down to the country lane at **Knighton**.

At the lane go left and then through a bridlegate on your right where there is a bridleway sign. The bridleway descends across open grass, with fine views of the fishing lake (and factory!). Go around the lake, over a bridge and follow the track up towards a copse. Bear left here and continue down to a gate. Go right, through the gate and follow a farm track up to Offley Grove Farm. At the lane go left and continue straight on along this through **Adbaston**, to arrive at the crossroads at **Outlands**. At this point you could do a little detour via Bishop's Offley to see the gorge, or alternatively, continue north along the pretty country lane until you arrive at the village of **Fairoak**. Although this is not off-road riding, there are very pleasant views of the little hills in this very quiet area.

Eventually you arrive at the village of Fairoak and, where the road bears right and climbs a little, you go left and down a gravel lane. At the bottom you go left again, and through a gate where it is signed as a bridleway to Hookgate. Follow the track up past a farm, through another gate and up the left-hand edge of a long field. Go through another gate and continue along the bottom of a field to yet a further gate and, after going through this, follow the obvious track, which bears left and around the hillock. This excellent track climbs steadily up past a wood and returns you to the farm and lane that you started out on. Follow the lane back to Hookgate and finally to the start in Ashley Heath.

Wellsbourne

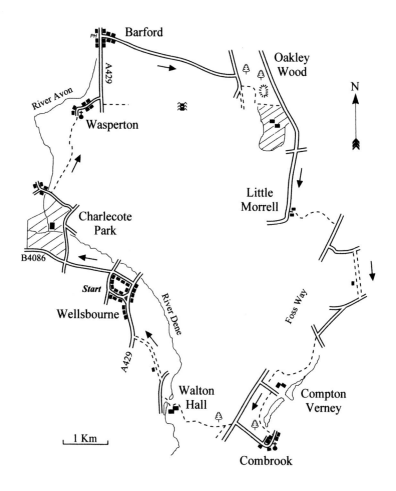

Barford

Oakley
Wood

River Avon

A429

Wasperton

Little
Morrell

Charlecote
Park

B4086

Start

Wellsbourne

River Dene

A429

Foss Way

Compton
Verney

Walton
Hall

Combrook

1 Km

N

Wellesbourne

Route Summary
Wellesbourne, Charlecote, Hampton Lucy, Wasperton, Oakley
Wood, Little Morrell, Lighthorne Rough, Compton Verney,
Combrook, Walton Hall. Wellesbourne.

Details
Grade – Moderate/Difficult
Time – 3 hr
Distance –   29km
    off road – 13km
    on road – 16km
Terrain – Parkland, fields and woods
Surface – Gravel and grass tracks, muddy in woods
Start Grid Reference – SP 277551
Maps – Stratford-upon-Avon, L151

Introduction
The landscape to the east of Stratford-upon-Avon is characterised by low lying, gently rolling arable country. Within this lie neat
little villages with thatched cottages, well ordered fields and scat-
tered prosperous country estates, of which there are a large number
in Warwickshire. Most of the off-road riding on this route is on good
bridleways and well-compacted tracks. There are short sections that
might cause difficulties, beside ploughed fields for example, but
these should be fairly easily overcome.

The route starts at Wellesbourne and almost immediately passes
the stately house and grounds of Charlecote Park, now owned by
the National Trust. The off-road riding starts at the village of Hampton Lucy, named after the Lucy family who originally owned the
Park, and passes through the quaint little village of Wasperton. From

here we go via Barford to Oakley Wood and then on to Compton Verney. The off-road riding here is either on good tracks or across parkland with only a short difficult section in a wood. After leaving the estate we pass through the pretty village of Combrook and then cross the Foss Way again. The following section, to Walton Hall, probably presents the real challenge of the route, involving difficult fields and woods, but is well worth the effort. From Walton Hall we return to the start via a good track and the main road into Wellesbourne.

Originally, the route (as described in the previous edition of this book) used a bridleway from Wasperton to Heathcote Farm and then via lanes to Oakley Wood. Unfortunately, the bridleway is only legal from the A429 up to the farm and there is no right of way for bikes (or horses) beyond that point. This has been the source of some aggravation for the farmer at Heathcote Farm, and the author requests that riders use the revised route outlined here.

Route Description

Take the **B4086** out of Wellesbourne towards Stratford and after about 1km go right for Charlecote. Go past the main entrance to the hall (too early to stop for a cream tea unfortunately!) and take the first left for Hampton Lucy. Just before you reach the mill there is a bridleway on the right. Go through a gate, into a field and follow the bridleway along the left-hand boundary across to a gate. After going through this bear slightly left to another small gate and a bridge over Thelsford Brook. Go left over the bridge and then bear right on a raised path, round past a plantation, to a good track. Take this, eventually arriving at a small lane that takes you into **Wasperton**. Follow the lane through the village until you reach the main A429. Go left here and continue along the main road for a little over a kilometre until you reach **Barford**, where you turn right opposite the Granville Arms and along Wasperton Lane. Follow the quiet country lane, until you reach a T-junction, where you go right.

After about 300 m the road bears right and a track to Ashorne continues straight on. Do not follow this but take a narrower bridleway that goes east around the edge of **Oakley Wood**. Follow this past Ashorne Hill College until you arrive at a road, where you go right. After just over 2 km you arrive at **Little Morrell**. Turn left down a drive (just before a right bend) and go past the farm, where you bear right and then left. After about 200 m the track opens out into a field, but you turn right and take a slightly less well defined track which follows the edge of the field and eventually leads round to a road, the **Foss Way**. This is the first time you encounter this ancient Roman road. Go right here, then left at the next junction for Lighthorne. Follow the road up and round past Bath Copse until you come to a track on the right for Far Westfields Farm. Go up this bridleway, through the gate at the farm (beware of the dogs) and down the drive to the road.

Turn right at the road and then fork next left down the hill to a T-junction with a track ahead. Go straight across and onto a good bridleway, which eventually leads onto the **Compton Verney** estate via a gate. Ahead you will see the house of Compton Verney, designed by Robert Adam in 1760, and surrounded by the landscape of 'Capability' Brown. The lakes together with the bridge were considered to be one of Brown's most beautiful stretches of naturalised water, and certainly look very grand on a fine day. Go up the track, admiring the view and bear right. At the top of the rise turn right through a gate, towards some farm buildings. Turn left past the farm and head straight for the lodge on the road. At the road, go left down the hill, until near the bottom you will see a sign for 'Park Farm' on the right. Go along this bridleway past the turning for Park Farm and then fork left through a gate by the side of a cattle grid and into a field. Bear left down the field, on a vague track to a gate that enters the wood by the lake. This location provides another excellent view of the old Compton Verney estate and lakes. Go into the wood (this can be difficult in the wet) and out the far side via another small gate. Follow the track down to a hollow and up the other side to arrive in the village by a row of pretty little cottages. This is the estate village of **Combrook**, built to replace the original village that was demolished when the park of Compton Verney was created. Turn right and go through the village, eventually forking left uphill to the main road, the Foss Way, again.

Go left at the road, then immediately right and down a track. At the bottom the track bears left but you (unfortunately!) continue straight on along the left-hand side of a field (with a ditch on your left) on an ill defined track, which leads into a wood. This can present some problems, particularly in the summer when the crops are well advanced, but persevere, as this is only a short section. Follow the track through the wood (soft in places), and then cut across a field and up to (at last!) a solid track at the top. Go left here and down to a gate, where you will have a fine view of **Walton Hall** ahead. Continue along the track, through another gate, bear left by some apartments and then continue past the 19th century hall and parish church. Follow the drive round, over the bridge and lakes to the road, where you go right. Take the second left along a track signposted 'The Old Rectory'. Continue past the houses, eventually arriving at the main **A429** where you turn right (take care!) and return to the start of the route in Wellesbourne.

The bridleway past Walton Hall

Henley-in-Arden

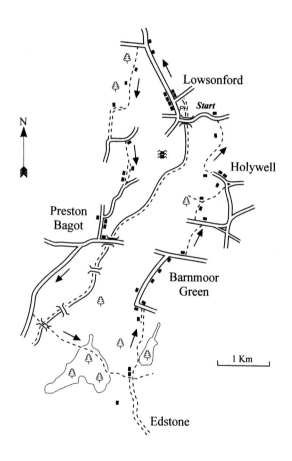

Lowsonford

Start

Holywell

N

Preston
Bagot

Barnmoor
Green

1 Km

Edstone

Henley-in-Arden

Route Summary

Lowsonford, Bushwood, Preston Fields, Preston Bagot, Preston Hill Farm, Barnmoor Green, Lye Green, Holywell, Lowsonford.

Details

Grade – Easy
Time – 2 1/2 hrs
Distance – 19km
    off road – 10km
    on road – 9km
Terrain – Gentle hills
Surface – Gravel tracks, but soft woodland bridleways
Start Grid Reference – SP 188678
Maps – Stratford-upon-Avon & surrounding area, L151.

Introduction

This attractive route is situated in the heart of the ancient Forest of Arden. Little of the original forest remains, but the area is wooded and the terrain gently undulating. A combination of bridleways and unclassified county roads makes for a relaxing ride with several pubs on the way, ideal for a summer evening. Most of the off-road is generally good, even after less than dry conditions, however the bridleway from Barnmoor Green to Yarningale can cause problems. This is well used by horses and, enclosed as it is by trees, can be extremely boggy. Discretion may be the better part of valour and a detour via Claverdon and Lye Green might be preferable.

Originally, the route (as described in the previous edition of this book) used the Stratford Canal from Preston Bagot to the rather superb aqueduct at Bearley. The tow-path was quite easy to ride but a little narrow in places and, unfortunately, British Waterways have since decided that this section of canal is not suitable for bikes. Please use the revised route outlined here.

Route Description

Start at Lowsonford by the interesting lock-keepers cottage on the Stratford-upon-Avon canal. Go north-east out of the village along the lane for Lapworth, and after about 1 km turn left for Henley and along Bushwood Lane. After a little over 100m you will see on the left the entrance to Bushwood Farm. Follow the gravel track, which is a bridleway, up past a house and a wood to the farm. A fenced-off track in front of the farmhouse leads you onto an excellent track. Enjoy a rattling good descent on a gravel track, which brings you to a small bridle gate. Follow the track round right and past Coppice Corner Farm to another bridle gate and onto the drive. Turn left on the drive, go over the disused railway bridge, and down to the road.

At the road turn left and after a short distance, where the road bears left by some houses, you go right and down a gravel track. Cross a superb little ford (use the bridge if you must!) and continue on up the track, which eventually brings you out at the end of a lane. Follow this lane down past some highly desirable residences to a junction, where you go straight on (right). The road descends a hill, past the Norman church at **Preston Bagot** and brings you to another junction, where you go left. Shortly, you arrive at the main A4189 road to Warwick, where you will eventually go right. However, 100m on your left you will see the impressive Manor House. This manor house and farm was built in 1550 by the order of the Earl of Warwick and was later the home of Ingram Bagot. Of more immediate importance perhaps, is the fact that at the end of the lane by the side of the manor house and adjacent to the Stratford canal is the Haven Tea Rooms! Although the author has not had the pleasure of experiencing this establishment, the refreshments on offer seem ideal for the sport of mountain biking!

To continue the route, we follow the A4189 towards Henley-in-Arden for a short distance. As the road starts to climb, you will see a lane on the left signposted 'Wootton Wawen'. Follow this for a little over a kilometre until you see a bridleway sign on the left. This delightful wooded track crosses over the Stratford canal and climbs steadily up through some woods. Exit the wood via a bridle gate and follow the track along the right-hand side of the field, then enjoy a steep little downhill to the farm. At this point you might want to do a little detour right taking you down to the tranquil lakes at **Edstone**. This section can hardly be described as off-road, but it is extremely pretty and quiet. Our route actually turns left at the farm, and then bears right and onto a gravel track which climbs up the shallow valley to a couple of gates. Take the right-hand gate and go along the left-hand side of the field on a good track to a further gate. Continue on a less distinct track across a pasture, through another gate and down a track to Chestnut Rise Farm. Bear right and down the lane to the road at Kington Grange, where you go left.

Follow the road until you reach the main road, where you go right. Fortunately, we do not stay on the road for long and, just past some houses on the left, there is a lane with a bridleway sign. This next section can pose problems! The wooded track, although a bridleway, tends to consider itself more a swamp than anything else, even after dry weather. After considerable struggling through bogs, the track improves and arrives at a lane, where you go left for Lye Green. An alternative, for those wishing to avoid this section, is to go right at Kington Grange, through Claverdon and then on to Lye Green. At Lye Green, fork left in the village and travel north towards Holywell. At the crossroads in **Holywell** take the left fork heading north-west on a dead-end road past some buildings. This eventually becomes a bridleway leading to a farm. Continue past the farm and bear right along a hedged bridleway, which descends to a small gate. Go through this and a further gate, to enter a field. Cross this diagonally left to a gate and up the right-hand side of the next field. After another gate follow the drive down to the road, where you go left and back to the start of the route in Lowsonford.

The ford at Prestonfield Lane

Above: *Lowsonford Lock*   Below: *Edstone*

Alcester

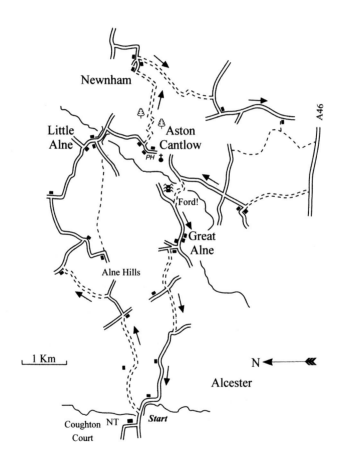

Newnham

Little
Alne

Aston
Cantlow

PH

Ford!

Great
Alne

Alne Hills

1 Km

N

Alcester

Coughton NT   *Start*
Court

A46

Alcester

Route Summary
Coughton Court, Alne Hills, Little Alne, Aston Cantlow, Newnham, Withycombe Wood, Great Alne, Coughton Court.

Details
Grade – Moderate/Difficult
Time – 3 hrs
Distance –   28km
    off road – 16km
    on road – 12km
Terrain – Some little hills
Surface – Some good grassy tracks, but also some muddy lanes, which can be difficult after rain.
Start Grid Reference – SP 087 603
Maps – Worcester, The Malverns & surrounding area L150, Strat ford-upon-Avon & surrounding area L151.

Introduction
The town of Alcester lies on the old Roman Ryknild Street, and the start of the route is about three miles to the north, at the National Trust property of Coughton Court. This great Tudor house has actually been the seat of the Throckmorton family since 1409 and has strong associations with the Gunpowder plot. The house is very interesting to visit and, of course, has an excellent tea-room! The lane to the south of the property fords the River Arrow, and there is limited parking by the ford. The route uses a variety of unclassified county roads and bridleways, the condition of the former being very much dependant on whether any 4x4s have recently passed through. The land rises to the north-east of Alcester around the Alne Hills, but generally the topography is fairly flat. The ease with which the

route can be completed is determined by the recent rainfall history. This is no more so than at the ford west of Aston Cantlow. This can be very difficult and if it is not possible to wade across it might be better to make a detour via Great Alne. Alternatively, you could just wait for the next Landrover!

Originally, the route was to include a bridleway from near Shelfield at SP 118 610 to Little Alne at SP 138 611. Although this is marked as a bridleway on the maps, it is in dispute locally. The author therefore recommends that it is not used and that the lanes to the north are used instead.

Route Description

Just to the south of Coughton Court is a little lane, which takes you down to a ford over the River Arrow. There is plenty of opportunity to park along this lane, and this is where the route starts. If the river is in flood, push your bike across the footbridge, otherwise cross the ford and immediately turn left through a gate and up a gravel track. This excellent unclassified county road climbs through National Trust parkland and up Windmill Hill. Rest at the top of this hill climb and enjoy the views back towards Coughton Court and over to Worcestershire. Continue along the track, eventually arriving at a lane at New End. Go right and then immediately left, for Shelfield Green.

The lane climbs and then, just as it starts to descend and bear right, you go left up a farm track which is signed as a bridleway. This is part of the ' Heart of England Way'. The track climbs steadily up past Alne Wood, through the woods, and then down the left-hand edge of a field. At the bottom of the field the bridleway goes left, along a wooded track and out onto a lane. Go right here and down to Shelfield Green, then left for Shelfield. At the T-junction go right for Little Alne, and then second left, over the River Alne and right for Aston Cantlow.

This is perhaps a good opportunity to have some refreshments at the King's Head in **Aston Cantlow**, but note the little track on your left just as you come into the village. Suitably refreshed you return to the track, another unclassified county road, which climbs gently towards some woods, and then climbs steeply up through them. This section can be a little tricky, due to overuse. At the top you continue down the left-hand edge of a field on a firmer grassy track. This excellent UCR crosses a field and then turns sharp left and leads up to the village of **Newnham**. Amble through the village and at the end you will see a lane on your right with a footpath sign and sign-posted 'Meadow Barn'. This is actually a bridleway and takes you past a house, on a dirt track, to a gate where there is a bridleway sign. At the end of the field the track becomes less distinct and continues along the left-hand edge of the next field on grassy track. Follow the bridleway around the edge of the field, right and then left, and up to a bridle gate. This last section can be difficult in wet weather. Things improve in the next field as you continue around the left-hand edge of the field and down to a rather muddy gate in some trees. Continue on a broad grassy track, which cuts across an arable field and soon brings you to a road.

Go right at the road and then left for Billesley. Continue on, ignoring the right turn for Great Alne and after about 1 km you will see a footpath sign on your right by some houses. This is a bridle-way and takes you up to Withycombe Wood. At this point you have two choices. You could go left and extend the route by following the field edge bridleway for about 1·5 kilometres until you reach the main **A46** at Red Hill. This bridleway can be difficult however, and the exit onto the road is awkward. A quick descent for a kilometre down the hill will bring you to a pleasant bridleway on the right, which will then take you back to the main route via Haselor and Walcote.

An easier alternative is to turn right at Withycombe Woods and follow around the edge of the wood, on a track that can be difficult after wet, until the bridleway dives into the woods and crosses to the other side. Eventually the track leaves the wood via a gate and then crosses a field and down to a road. Go left here and after a little over a kilometre you come to a crossroads. At this point you have two choices. If there has been a great deal of rain, you might like to avoid the next section by continuing straight on for **Great Alne**. For those who fancy a bit of fun, turn right for Aston and continue along Mill Lane. As the road bears right you go left where it is signed 'Unsuitable for Motor Vehicles'. This dirt track, which is an unclassified county road, takes you down to a rather large ford, which can only really be crossed after a dry spell of weather. Wade (or try to ride!) across or alternatively, wait until some Landrovers appear and cadge a lift (thanks guys, I take back what I said about 4x4s!). After the fun, continue up a little lane, which brings you out onto the B4089.

At the road go left and continue for less than a kilometre to Great Alne. Take a right turn down Park Lane and go straight on where it says 'No Through Road'. Just past the last house on your left you will see a green lane. Even after a brace of Landrovers had been through here, the track was still in reasonable riding condition. Eventually the track improves and brings you to a road, which you cross over and onto another track. This slightly rutted track brings you down to a lane, where you go right. Wend your way along the lane through Coughton Fields, ford the River Arrow, and arrive back at the start at Coughton Court. With luck you will just be in time to have a refreshing cup of tea, if they will let you in!

Coughton Court National Trust

Chipping Campden

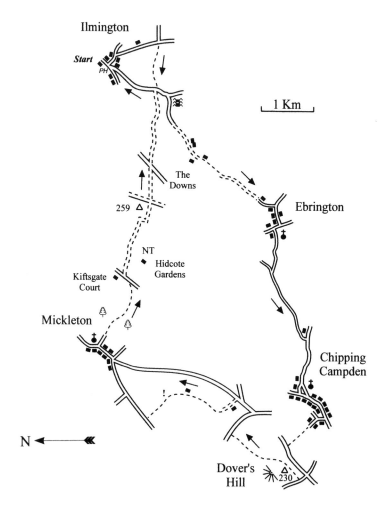

Ilmington

Start

PH

1 Km

The Downs

259 △

NT
◆ Hidcote Gardens

Kiftsgate Court

Mickleton

Ebrington

Chipping Campden

Dover's Hill

230

N ◀━━━◄

Chipping Campden and Hidcote

Route Summary
Ilmington, Foxcote, Ebrington, Chipping Campden, Dover's Hill, Dairy Hills, Mickleton, Kiftsgate Court, Hidcote Manor, Nebsworth, Ilmington.

Details
Grade – Difficult
Time – 3 hrs
Distance –   27km
     off road – 15km
     on road – 12km
Terrain – Hills
Surface – Good well-drained hilly grass/pebble tracks
Start Grid Reference – SP 213 434
Maps – Stratford-upon-Avon, L151

Introduction
    The Ilmington Downs, as they are known locally, form the highest point in Warwickshire at a height of 259 metres above sea level. Situated in the far southwest of the county, they allude to an altogether different kind of terrain from that found in the rest of Warwickshire. Here you will find more than just a hint of the hilly Cotswold country to the south and, although separated from them, the downs can be considered as the northern-most outlier of the Cotswolds. The route starts in the charming village of Ilmington, climbs round the eastern flanks of the downs and drops down into Chipping Campden by way of Ebrington. From here, a stiff climb takes us up onto Dover's Hill escarpment, to be rewarded with fine panoramic views of the Vale of Evesham. The hill derives its name from Robert Dover who in the early 1600s created the 'Cotswold

Olympick Games' there. These games proved so popular and bois-
terous that they had to be banned in the nineteenth century, due to
riots in Chipping Campden. At any rate the hill is safe now and the
bridleway provides a fun and sporting descent! A slightly tricky bridleway over Dairy Hills brings us to Mickleton, and then the hard
work starts. An increasingly steep bridleway climbs up past first,
Kiftsgate Court garden and then, Hidcote Manor and Gardens. Pretty
flowers may not be your most important consideration at this stage,
but at least the National Trust do refreshments at Hidcote. Still more
climbing takes us over the Ilmington Downs and then back home.

Route Description

Leave the charming little Cotswold village of Ilmington via the
little road for Shipston, opposite the Red Lion pub. Shortly after
leaving the village go right for Compton Scorpion and past Harolds
Farm. At the junction of a road from the left, you go right and across
a field to a gate. Ascend the steep hill, eventually arriving at a gate,
which leads onto a road. Resist the temptation to carry straight on,
this is our return route, but go left and along the lane. After only
300m bear right, where it is signed 'Foxcote House and Farm Only
- Private Drive'. This is in fact a bridleway, although you would
find that hard to believe. Is this the only bike route ever devised that
has an electrically operated bridle gate? Press the button and get
yourself captured on video - the locals are a little security conscious
around here! The drive leads towards the very impressive early eight-
eenth century mansion, where we bear right and go down hill. Climb
up past some houses and barns and continue straight on along side
an arable field on a good track. The track enters another field, bears
left and down, then right at the bottom and up past some farm buildings. The track eventually becomes metalled and leads into another
charming Cotswold village, **Ebrington**.

At the T-junction, go right and follow the main road through the little village, heading for Chipping Campden. After a couple of kilometres, turn left onto the B4035 and follow the one way system into **Chipping Campden**. Go left onto the main street and, where the main road bears left, continue straight on for Weston-sub-Edge. Take the next right past the church. The road bears round to the right, but we go left and up Hoo Lane, on the Cotswold Way. The tarmac gives out and becomes a track which climbs up Dover's Hill to a road, where we go left and along to a crossroads. Turn right here and climb the hill. At the top of the hill on the right is the Dover's Hill carpark.

Dover's Hill is one of the highlights of the trip, so have a picnic, enjoy the view and then prepare to have fun! Go through the bridle gate along the Cotswold Way, keeping to the boundary on the right-hand side. Follow this round to a gate and through this into a small wood. Follow the obvious track out onto open ground and then enjoy a rattling good descent to the road. At the road turn right, then first left and after about 400m you come to a fork in the roads. Ignore the roads and go left down a bridleway signposted 'Private Road'. Just after some farm buildings on the left there is a bridleway sign on the right, which takes you into the trees. This actually runs parallel to the road but is a lot more fun (and it's legal). The wood and track end at a gate, where you continue across the field straight ahead. Negotiate three more gates to eventually come to Middle Norton Farm. Cross the farm track (which actually leads to the road but is not a right of way) and aim to the left, past some woods to a small bridle gate on the far side of the field. This can be difficult in the wet and there is no clear indication of where the track goes. If and when you reach the gate, go through this and down the side of the field, eventually coming to the road previously mentioned. (If the weather has been very wet you might want to just continue straight on for **Mickleton** at the fork in the roads mentioned above.)

Go right at the road and into Mickleton. Just before the church turn right, go up a lane and through a bridle gate between the grave-yards. Cross the field, bearing right to another bridle gate and a stream. Follow the woods and stream to yet another gate and up the edge of the field to a small gate on the right. This takes you into the **Kiftsgate Court** Estate. Continue up an increasingly steep hill, un-til you reach a country lane. After having a much needed rest, cross over the lane and continue on up past the entrance and carpark of **Hidcote Gardens** (tea stop?) to a gravel track straight ahead. Fol-low this to the top of the hill and eventually a road. Cross over and follow the track down by the side of the field, through the wood, and across a field and down to a small bridle gate in the far left-hand corner. Cross over the road and climb up a sandy track past some radio masts. Enjoy the view of the Midland plain to the north, and then continue through some woods and finally down to the small road that we started out on. Turn left here and return to the village by a steep descent on road, but make sure your brakes are still work-ing first!

Ilmington Downs

Broadway

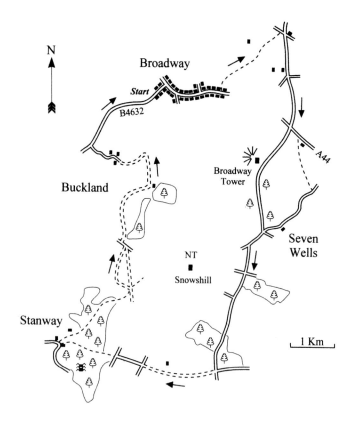

N

Broadway

Start

B4632

Buckland

Broadway
Tower

NT
Snowshill

Seven
Wells

Stanway

A44

1 Km

Broadway

Route Summary
Broadway, Buckle Street, Taddington, Lidcombe Wood, Shenberrow Hill, Laverton Hill, Buckland.

Details
Grade – Difficult
Time – 3 hours
Distance – 27km
    off road – 13km
    on road – 14km
Terrain – Hills
Surface – Parkland, fields, woodland tracks and hard pack
Start Grid Reference – SP 096375
Maps – Worcester and The Malverns, L150.

Introduction
This route starts in the centre of the picturesque little town of Broadway, which on a fine summers day, and particularly at weekends, can be almost overrun by day-trippers. The sight of a mudsplattered mountain biker at the end of a long hard day can have the effect of causing some mild amusement amongst these less energetic folk! Fortunately, the route soon escapes the hustle and bustle of the town and climbs steeply via parkland up onto the Cotswold escarpment, from where there is a superb view to the west. The route tracks south, using a combination of quiet Cotswold lanes and a RUPP section of the Ryknild Street, an old Roman road much fallen into disuse. After turning west down a pleasant little unclassified road the fun really starts. A superb descent through woods is followed by an energy-sapping climb back up onto Shenberrow Hill. The reward is an exhilarating ride along the crest of the hill on an

excellent RUPP. The views to the west and north are stunning on a clear day. Look out for the National Trust's Snowshill Manor, a 15th century house and gardens well worth a visit, with an interesting museum of unusual collections. After about 4 km, the track leads down into the sleepy village of Buckland and back to Broadway.

An alternative route for those who prefer an almost completely off-road experience is also possible, although I have not tried all of it myself. Start at Buckland, climb the steep hill and follow the RUPP along the east side of Laverton Hill to Great Brockhampton Farm and then a T-junction. A right turn followed by a left will take you along a bridleway to a road junction where you turn left to Welsh-man's Hedge Wood. Here you follow the bridleway through and along the side of the wood to a road, where a right turn will bring you to the unclassified county road mentioned in the main route description. Here you follow the route back to Buckland via the woods down to Stanway or, if you want to make life somewhat easier, along the RUPP from Stanway Ash Wood and over Shenberrow and Laverton Hill. Total distance is about 15 km, only 2 km on road.

Route Description

Start in the centre of Broadway, heading east along the main A44. As the road begins to climb near the edge of the town, there is a lane on the left signed 'Willersey and Saintbury Church'. Grate-fully leaving the noise of the town, follow the lane past some houses to a white bridle gate on the right, just where the track bears left. This is where the hard work begins! Cross the short stretch of field to a gap, bear right to another gate and then left uphill on the obvi-ous grassy track. Go through another gate and continue by the side of a new plantation to the open ground. Bear right uphill and cross the parkland following the obvious grassy track. At the top left-hand corner is a gate in some trees, through which you continue on and up to a drive. Cross this and bear left to a gate. The bridleway now weaves its way through trees and bushes at the bottom of the

Golf Course. Resist the temptation to actually ride on the course, because not only is this illegal and possibly dangerous, it is also cheating! Continue along the good track (soft in places) until you arrive at a small lane, where you go right.

Turn right at the crossroads and climb up hill to a junction, where you go right (straight on) for Snowshill along the old Buckle Street. This lane is thought to be Neolithic in origin and the name may derive from Saxon, meaning beacon, as the road traverses the tops of the hills. At the main **A44** from Broadway go left (take care!) and after only 300 m turn right where there is a bridleway sign near a house. Pass through a gate and into a long grassy field to another gate at the far end. Go through this and continue down a narrow track by the side of the field to the bottom, where it becomes wider. This is the old Roman road, the Ryknild Street, which leads to a road where you go right. The Ryknild Street does continue to Spring Hill House, but unfortunately is no longer a right of way. Follow the road up past **Seven Wells** and eventually bear left for Stow and Bourton on the Water. The lanes in this area are very quiet and on a fine day, the high plateau of the Cotswolds is extremely pleasant. Go over a crossroads and down hill, continuing straight on where a road comes in from the right, and climb uphill steadily towards some woods. Although this section may not be the most challenging of biking, the rewards of your efforts are soon to arrive.

As the road leaves the wood you will see a road on your left and on your right a track signed 'Unsuitable for Motors' (SP 104314). Go right and down past the edge of the wood on this excellent track. This crosses a stream at Dirty Bridge and then continues up to a road junction. Carry straight on up a narrow lane for **Stanway** towards the woods at the top and another junction. At this point it would be possible to go right where it is signed 'Unsuitable for Motors' to join our route at a later stage. This would, however, make life far too easy and would also miss one of the delights of the route! Continue straight on into the wood, following a bridle sign, to arrive at a large gate which is the entrance to the Stanway Estate. There now follows a rattling good decent through the woods on excellent track, with many bumps and a few rocks, all the way to the bottom. Resist any temptation to branch left or right, as these are not rights of way, but continue down until you arrive at some houses.

Unfortunately, all good things come to an end and usually they have to be paid for! Just before you reach the road there is a narrow lane which doubles back up to your right. Although this starts off quite steeply and can be very soft, it soon levels out. This is the start of a reasonably gentle but interesting little climb all the way back up onto the Cotswold plateau. The scenery here is quite delightful and the climbing never too hard to spoil the fun. The track widens and follows the edge of the wood to arrive at a pool. Go straight on following the bridleway sign, past a hidden reservoir and noisy pumps (if running) continuing up hill. The track climbs steadily and then finally becomes short and steep, arriving at the edge of the woods by a farm. Bear left along the edge of the woods until, where the track bears right and leaves the woods (footpath only), you carry straight on through a small gate and into a small field. Cross this diagonally right to a green gate, carry on across a similar field to another green gate and onto a large track. This is in fact a RUPP that follows the top of Shenberrow Hill. Go left and follow the excellent track, admiring the views, until you arrive at a gate, which leads onto a lane. Go left for about 100 m or so until you see a sign on your right saying 'Cotswold Way'. Follow this, through a gate and again along the RUPP, with an excellent view of Broadway ahead. The track goes downhill, past a bridleway on the left and down to a gate with a blue bridleway marker. Continue along the firm track, through another gate with a marker, to arrive at a barn. This is in fact the junction of another RUPP. Go left through a gate and along a solid track. After a while the track bears round to the left, becomes metalled and quickly descends into the very pretty village of **Buckland**. Carry on through the village to the B4632 where you turn right and return to Broadway.

RUPP towards Buckland – The Cotswold Way

Bredon & Dumbleton

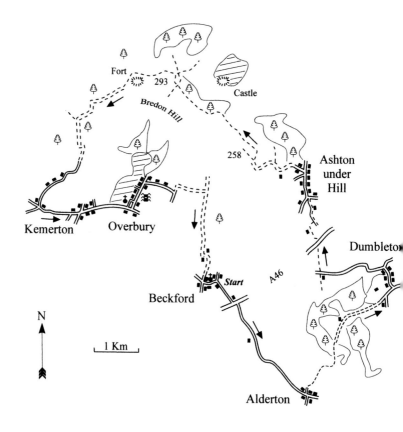

Fort

293

Bredon Hill

Castle

258

Ashton under Hill

Kemerton

Overbury

Dumbleton

Beckford

Start

A46

N

1 Km

Alderton

Bredon and Dumbleton

Route Summary
Beckford, Alderton, Dumbleton, Ashton under Hill, Bredon Hill,
Kemerton, Overbury, Beckford.

Details
Grade – Very difficult
Time – 4 Hrs
Distance –   30km
    off road – 18km
    on road – 12km
Terrain – Hills
Surface – Mostly good gravel tracks
Start Grid Reference – SO 976357
Maps – Malvern Hills and Bredon Hill Explorer 14, Worcester,
The Malverns & surrounding area, L150

Introduction
   Bredon Hill, situated in the county of Worcestershire, is what is
geologically called an outlier. Here the Cotswold limestone beds
have been raised and folded by prehistoric forces and then eroded
over the passage of time. The result is a hill that presents two different facets. To the south, the land slopes away gently along the plane
of the beds, whilst the northern flank of the hill is much steeper. The
hill is almost 1000ft high and although separate, is considered to be
part of the Cotswolds. There are numerous bridleways, footpaths
and old tracks crossing the hill, many in excellent condition. This
route links together the smaller but even prettier hills to the south-
east, of Alderton and Dumbleton, and although this involves a little
riding on small lanes, the excursion is well worthwhile. For those
who prefer an almost complete off-road experience it is possible to

contrive a route that climbs and descends Bredon hill three times, via Ashton, Elmley Castle, Kemerton and Overbury. This involves over 2000 ft of climbing, which is unusual for mountain biking in the Midlands!

Route Description

Starting by the church in the centre of the village of Beckford, go east and follow the road round to the right, soon arriving at the main **A46**. Taking care, do a dogleg left then right for **Alderton**. This quiet lane soon takes you away from the traffic and after a couple of kilometres you arrive at the village itself. As you enter the village, just before the Gardeners Arms pub, there is a track with a bridleway sign on the left. Follow this out of the village, up the side of a couple of fields and towards the woods. Go through a gate and straight on into the woods, ignoring the tracks to the left and right. Climb up the steep track through these very pretty woods, which can also be quite difficult after a period of wet. At the top you arrive at a track where you go left to a large gate. This bridleway takes you down past Hill Farm to the village of **Dumbleton**. The views at this point are really spectacular, but take care. Watch your speed as you descend – the track has speed bumps, which can take you by surprise (we speak from painful experience!). Follow the track down past Dumbleton Hall with its lake on the left, to the main gate. Go left, along the lane and then left again into the village. Follow the road through the village, bearing left at the end. After a little over 1 km you will see, opposite a house, a grassy bridleway on your right. Go through the large gates and follow the track to the main road again.

At the main road go right and then immediately left through a small gate, where there is a bridleway sign. Follow this track down to the drive of a caravan site and on towards the reception (!). Bear right and go around the back of the site where there is a blue way-marker. The track takes you to a small gate, through which you go right, along the edge of a field on a good track, arriving eventually at a lane. Follow Back Lane into the village of **Ashton under Hill**, where you go left and then turn right for Elmley Castle. Continue up the main street, stopping off at the Star pub if you are in need of refreshments, until you see Cottons Lane on the left. This metalled lane soon becomes a bridleway and enters some trees. Go through a gate, and climb up past a farm to another gate. Climb more steeply on a rocky track to yet another gate and then to a division of the ways. Go left, through a gate and up the right-hand side of the field. This track is ill defined, but at the top you join a definite track, where you go left. This takes you through a gate and round the hill to the right. Just around the corner the track divides and you continue straight on (right), following the bridleway sign indicating that you are on the Wychavon Way. At the top is a gate, through which you turn right and follow the edge of an arable field round to the left. This excellent track climbs very gently now, so take time to admire the views to the southeast of the Cotswolds and closer to hand, Dumbleton Hill.

Continue climbing along the good track and after going through a gate, along side another arable field. Further on still there are fine views on your right of the Vale of Evesham and of Evesham itself. Go through another gate and continue alongside trees. This excellent track passes near a communications tower and eventually you will see a bridle gate which enters a wood. For those who like to spice things up a little, it is possible to take this track down into the wood, turn sharp left as you leave the wood and then return to the original route, after a stiff little hill climb. We continue straight on, soon arriving at a copse on the left and a gate. The steep nature of the northern flank of **Bredon Hill** now becomes apparent. Carrying straight on along the right-hand side of grazing land we arrive at Bredon Hill fort. Keep to the wall on the right (the fort itself is NOT a right of way to bikes), but notice the double ditch that surrounds the fort. When the Iron Age fort was excavated, apparently the mutilated bodies of fifty men were discovered. These last defenders of the fort had not been buried, but had presumable been left where they fell. Not perhaps a good place to visit at night! As you follow the wall round to the left you pass the Banbury Stone, considered by some to be a Druid sacrificial stone, and then a tower, called Parsons Folly. The track passes the double ditch again, goes through a gate and starts to descend towards some woods.

Enter the deciduous wood via a gate and then continue by the side of the woods on an excellent sandy track with good views to the south. Eventually you arrive at a small gate, through which you turn left and go down the left-hand side of a couple of fields. Notice the superb view of the Malvern Hills on your right. Continue down hill, bearing left past the end of the copse, onto an obvious track. Follow the track down past another clump of trees and bear left to a gate. Follow the gravel track right and down hill. Eventually the track becomes metalled and bears right, continuing down to the village of Lower Westmancote.

In the village you arrive at a T-junction, where you go left for Kemerton and Overbury. Although not strictly necessary, a detour north through the village of **Kemerton** is well worthwhile, as the village is particularly attractive. On arriving at **Overbury** take the first left, up past the church and round to the main street, where you go left. As you climb up hill note the entrance to Overbury Park on your left. This is in fact a bridleway that will take you back up to the top of Bredon Hill. We, however, carry on up to the top of the village and turn first right. Follow the lane out of the village and where it goes sharp right, we turn left up a gravel track. Soon the track splits and you bear right, go over a small stream and climb the hill. At the top of the climb you arrive at a junction. Go right and follow the track down hill to a farm. Go left through the farmyard and then right and onto a metalled lane, which takes you down to the village of Beckford. At the junction go right for Alderton and back to the start of the route.

The bridleway down to Westmancote

Suckley Hills

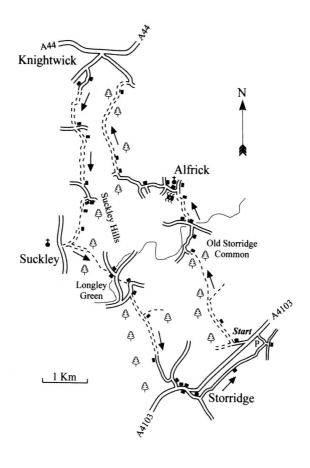

N

Knightwick

A44

A44

Alfrick

Suckley Hills

Old Storridge
Common

Suckley

Longley
Green

A4103

Start

P

1 Km

Storridge

A4103

A4103

Suckley Hills

Route Summary
Leigh Sinton(2km west of), Old Storridge Common, Alfrick, Crews Hill, Knightwick, Suckley, Storridge, Crumpton Hill, Leigh Sinton(west of).

Details
Grade – Difficult
Time – 3 hrs
Distance –   24km
    off road – 14km
    on road – 10km
Terrain – Lots of ups and downs.
Surface – Some soft woodland tracks, but many excellent stony/ rocky tracks.
Start Grid Reference – SO 765 497
Maps – Worcester, The Malverns & surrounding area L150, Hereford, Leominster & surrounding area L149.

Introduction
The Malverns are renowned for the annual Malverns Classic MTB festival and the hills are also justifiably popular with walkers. The whole area can be seething with tourists and visitors at weekends, yet just a few miles to the north lies an area that seems almost forgotten in time. This secluded area of Worcestershire is rich in footpaths, bridleways and unclassified county roads. Add the magic ingredients of hills and woods and you have the perfect recipe for some excellent off-road riding. The start of the route may not be auspicious, being at a large pull-in on the busy A4103 just a couple of kilometres southwest of Leigh Sinton. However, the easy bridleway to Old Storridge Common soon leaves the busy world behind.

There then follows a challenging hill climb up Sandy Lane to the village of Alfrick, and after a section of road we join the Worcestershire Way, with a scenic descent to Knightwick. A series of solid UCRs brings us to Suckley, followed by a couple of hill climbs to Storridge. Finally, a speedy ride along a back lane brings us back to the start of the route. A challenging day out in pretty countryside, with some excellent hill climbs and descents.

Route Description

The route starts at a large lay-by on the Worcester – Hereford **A4103**, just 2km west of the village of Leigh Sinton. Take the main road in the Hereford direction for a short distance, and then fork right, where there is a lane with a 'No Through Road' sign. After a short distance turn right at a farm, where there is a 'Private Road' sign. This is in fact a bridleway. Follow the farm lane up towards The Norrest, past the farm and barn conversions, and on to a stony track towards some woods. After 0·5 km bear left through a gate where there is a bridleway sign and into a field. Continue along the bottom of this field following the indistinct bridleway. This takes you through the wood to another gate. Cut straight across the field, with rising pasture land to your left, to arrive at another gate into more woods. The track through the delightful woods can be rather chopped up, but after bearing left brings you down to a lane by some houses.

At the lane go right, down the hill to a T-junction, where you go right again and continue on down to a road. Go left here, over a bridge, and then immediately right by a house. The stony track forks left after about 100 m and follows alongside a stream. This excellent track, Sandy Lane, climbs steeply up through some woods, ascending an interesting rock staircase, and is probably more of a challenge going up, than coming down – but well worth a try! Eventually you arrive at a farm, which you pass through and out onto a lane. Follow the tarmac lane down to a junction, where you go left.

The road climbs slightly, then descends steeply, only to climb up again to the top of Crews Hill. At the top you will see a lane on your right, which is a bridleway. This is the Worcestershire Way. Follow this past some houses, bear left and continue along the tree-lined track, which can be chopped up in places. Bear left again at the Rhododendrons and continue along a delightful woodland track. Eventually the wood clears a little on your right, giving superb views to the east. The track continues through the woods along the ridge, and after going through a couple of bridle gates, you come out into the open, with beautiful views to the west. Carry on along the ridge, through a couple more bridle gates and along the left-hand side of a field. Continue through yet more bridle gates, along the top left-hand edge of the field, descending slightly. This is a splendid location with superb views all around. After arriving at another bridle gate you enter a wood and exit via another gate. Follow the ridge along the top to a small bridle gate, down a wooded track and past a house. The stony road leads down to a tarmac lane and to a junction. What a superb section you have just completed!

At the T-junction go left for **Knightwick** and, just before you get to the main A44, go left again for **Suckley**. After a short distance go left up a small lane past a pretty little church. The lane becomes pot-holed and gently climbs back towards the hills. Eventually the road gives up and becomes a muddy track. Continue straight on at a gate, following the track around the bottom of a field and up to a farm. After another gate you go straight on through the yard and along a lane to a crossroads by some houses. Cross over and continue along a track, past a farm and down to a gate. The route continues across pasture land on a good stony track to arrive at another gate. The good tree-lined track eventually arrives at some houses and to a road. Go left here, then first right in front of some white cottages where there is a bridle way sign. This takes you past a pink(!) cottage, then along a narrow track, through a gate and into a field. Continue on, bearing slightly right and towards a house, through a small bridle gate and onto a lane. Follow this and, after going over a little stream, go left through a gate and across a field. After another gate, climb uphill and towards the woods. The track up through the woods is steep and difficult, so you may need to get off and push here. Eventually you reach the top and then you can enjoy a fun descent down to a gate, across a field and onto a lane via another gate at Tundridge. Follow the lane past some pretty oast houses and down to a road.

At the road go right and, after a short distance, you will see a steep lane on your left. Follow this up to the top, to arrive at a house and lane. Go right, down the hill and immediately after a black and white cottage go left where there is a Worcestershire Way bridle way sign. This climbs gradually on a stony track, goes through a gate and along a farm track towards a farm. Continue along the lane which, after a right turn, eventually takes you to the **A4103**. Go left here and then immediately right along the B4219 for Malvern. Take the first left and follow the little lane over Crumpton Hill. A final left turn at a junction brings us back to the main road and the start of the route.

View from bridleway over Birch Wood

Kinver

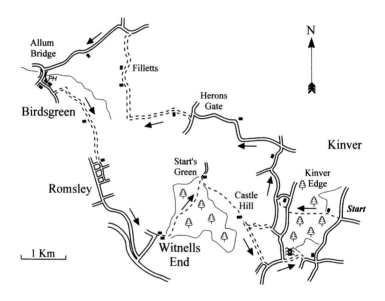

Allum
Bridge

Filletts

PH

Birdsgreen

Herons
Gate

Kinver

Start's
Green

Castle
Hill

Kinver
Edge

Start

Romsley

1 Km

Witnells
End

Kinver, and beyond!

Route Summary
Kinver Edge, Sheepwash Lane, Herons Gate, Filletts, Birdsgreen, Bowhills, Romsley, Witnells End, Arley Wood, Kingsford, Kinver Edge.

Details
Grade – Difficult
Time – 3 hrs
Distance – 26km
    off road – 14km
    on road – 12km
Terrain – Hilly
Surface – Generally firm bridleways and tracks
Start Grid Reference – SO 835 821
Maps – Wyre Forest & Kidderminster – Bridgnorth E218, Kidderminster & Wyre Forest area L138.

Introduction
The thickly wooded scarp of Kinver Edge has long been popular with sightseers and walkers. Many paths and tracks wend their way through the dense woodland that envelops the soft sandstone edge. The eastern side of the edge rises gently, but then dramatically drops away to the west, revealing glimpses of the quiet and gentle landscape beyond. Although there are permissive horse riding routes along the edge, these are strictly for horses, not bikes. There is, however, an excellent bridleway that climbs the gentle eastern side of the edge, and then plummets down the western scarp. A severe test of downhill skills! Although initially the route involves a little bit of road work, this is along very quiet country lanes and is followed by an excellent farm track over to Birdgreen. A combination of ancient

green lanes and forestry tracks returns us to the start of the route, with splendid views of Kinver Edge as the finale.

Route Description

The route starts at the carpark on the east side of Kinver Edge, on the border of Worcestershire and Staffordshire. The bridleway follows the drive up towards Kinver Edge Farm. However, most people (including horses and bikes) follow the broad sandy track, which climbs steadily in a westerly direction, up through the woods. Actually, this can be a bit of a challenge in itself, as the track is initially very sandy and can be quite fun to try and ride. The track soon reaches the top of the edge, at a picnic spot and waymarker, and the true nature of Kinver Edge becomes apparent. The eastern flanks of the edge are quite tame and rise gently to the top, but the western flanks are altogether different, falling away very steeply.

The next section needs a little bit of a health warning. Whilst not particularly difficult for experts, beginners should take care! Continue straight on at the old oak tree, down a very steep and narrow track which hairpins through the woods, down the west side of the Edge. Watch out for the log and rock steps, which make excellent little drop-offs, or brilliant places to do face plants, depending on how your luck goes! Whatever you do, take care and look out for horses and walkers. If you get down in one piece, you'll probably want to go back up for another try! At any rate, continue straight on, following the blue waymarkers, and eventually you will arrive at the Kingswood carpark on the other side of Kinver Edge.

At the road go right, until after a couple of hundred metres you see a bridleway on the left. This narrow, slightly overgrown lane does not look inviting, but actually presents few problems. The bridleway bears right and soon arrives at a country lane. Go left here to the crossroads and then right. This charming little lane, called Sheepwash Lane, provides an opportunity for a little rest and a chance to admire Kinver Edge to your right. Bear right at Beacon Lane and then left at the crossroads for Romsley.

After an easy ride along the country lane for a couple of kilometres you come to a T-junction, where you go left. After 100 m take the rocky farm track on the right, which is a bridleway. The track takes you up to Howlet Hall farm. Fortunately, the bridleway has been diverted here and now goes round to the back of the farm and continues along the track. This excellent solid track travels west for a kilometre and then, by some woods, turns right. A couple more kilometres of easy off-road riding follows, as the track takes you past the duck pond at Perry House and the very smart looking **Filletts**. Eventually you arrive at the road, where you go left.

Although the next section is on-road, it does provide a fast and furious descent to **Allum Bridge**. If you can take your eyes off the road for long enough, you will see ahead the village of Highly, on the opposite side of the Severn Valley. At the bottom of the hill go over the bridge, past the Inn and first left for Romsley. Just after leaving the village you will see a rocky little lane on your left. This track has recently been upgraded to a bridleway and links to a long bridleway (which was a RUPP) which runs in a south-easterly direction, parallel to the road. Although this can be difficult in places, this next section is well worth the off-road challenge! After an initially rocky start the lane bears right and becomes a bit narrow and over-grown, but push on as it does improve. The lane widens into a hedged farm track that climbs gently, passes through a couple of farm gates and arrives at Bowhills, a grand but rather dilapidated farmhouse. Continue on an excellent stony farm track, which unfortunately narrows, but eventually opens out and leads into the hamlet of **Romsley**.

Continue straight on along the tarmac back lane, and then bear right and up to the road. Go left here, following the road for about a kilometre and a half, until it descends to a junction near the A442 at Bellman's Cross. Go left here for Kinver and down the hill. As the road bears left, you go right for the hamlet of **Witnell's End**.

Follow the stony track past the farms and into the woods. Where the track hairpins right, you continue straight on where there is a bridleway sign. This track, which is used by horses, is mostly good and provides a little bit of a technical descent, until it arrives at a stream, where a spare pair of wellies would probably be very useful! At this point the bridleway joins a forestry track, and you go left. Follow this excellent and easy gravel road as it climbs gently, until eventually you exit Shatterford Wood (Forest Enterprise).

Continue up the access track until you almost reach **Starts Green** Farm. Just before the property, doubling back to your right, is a narrow and rather hidden bridleway. This is easily missed, as it does not quite agree with the maps, but if you look carefully, you will see the blue waymarkers. If you're standing in front of the entrance to the house, you've gone too far! Follow the overgrown bridleway, which can be rather soft to begin with, but soon opens out into a fantastic track with stupendous views. I exaggerate not! On a fine summer evening the views from this track are hard to beat. To the right you will see the woods that you have just passed through, and way to the south, the Malverns. On your left, wooded Kinver Edge stands proud with Vale's Rock clearly visible, and Birmingham glinting and lurking in the distance. Hard to believe that you can be in such fine countryside, and yet be so close to a major conurbation. The hedged track follows along the top of a broad ridge towards **Castle Hill**. Bear left by the farm, go through a small bridle gate, across a pasture, through another gate and onto a gravel lane. Follow this dead straight bridleway down the hill, until you reach the road.

Go left at the road, and then, where the road bears left, continue straight on along a sandy bridleway. This is a sting in the tail, as this very sandy track is nigh on impossible to ride. Local riders obviously use the woods, but this is not legal. Eventually the track bears right and arrives at a lane. Go left into Blakeshall, then left again for Kinver. Follow the road and soon you arrive back at the carpark.

Kinver locals – looking for some downhill

Wyre Forest

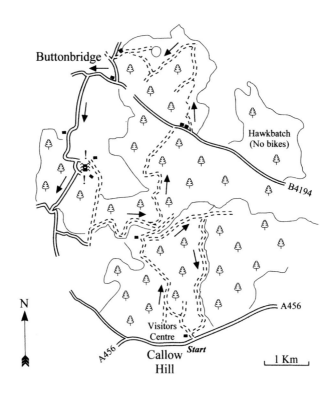

Buttonbridge

Hawkbatch
(No bikes)

B4194

N

A456

Visitors
Centre

Start

A456

Callow
Hill

1 Km

Wyre Forest

Route Summary
Wyre Forest Visitors Centre, Park House, Buttonoak, Buttonbridge, Sturt Common, Dowles Brook, Disused Railway, Wyre Forest Visitors Centre.

Details
Grade – Moderate
Time – 2 1/2 hours
Distance – 25km
    off road – 19km
    on road – 6km
Terrain – Hilly
Surface – Good forestry tracks
Start Grid Reference – SO 750740
Maps – Wyre Forest & Kidderminster E 218, Kidderminster & Wyre Forest area L138

Introduction
The Wyre Forest is a justifiably popular area with walkers and mountain bikers alike, being so close to the south-west of Birmingham, and yet seemingly to be divorced from the hustle and bustle of modern life. The Forestry Commission have not encouraged mountain biking in the forest in the past but recently, recognising peoples desire to enjoy the woods on bikes, they have devised a zoning scheme to ensure that conflicts are kept to a minimum. They have created a bike route in the main block, as well as way-marked and separate routes for walkers and horse riders. A horseshoe waymarker does not indicate a bridleway and must not be used by bikers, unless it coincides with a gravelled road. Generally speaking, in the main area of woodland, bikers are allowed to use the main gravelled tracks

and public bridleways. Bike access is not permitted in the Hawkbatch area. However, there is an open access policy in the North Kinlet area, "where all roads, rides and paths may be used".

In devising this route I have attempted to create a route which is a little more challenging than the standard amble through the forest. The route starts at the visitor Centre at Callow Hill and uses the bridleway north, crosses the B4194 and enters the North Kinlet block. The riding in this area is more technical and demanding and the precise route can really be worked out on the spot - just make sure you have a compass! The return is via Buttonbridge and Sturt Common, where you will note a couple of lanes, which lead to a dead-end RUPP (marked as a bridleway). The status of these lanes is unclear, as many users view the lane into Kingswood as a right of way, but unfortunately the locals do not! Our route therefore continues south and re-enters the forest at Dowles Brook, returning to the visitor centre via the dismantled railway and the Forest Enterprise bike route.

Route Description

Start at the Callow Hill visitors' centre. Follow the main gravel track north down the hill into the forest. After a short distance you take the left-hand fork (straight on), up the hill. Follow the forestry road until you come to a T-junction, where you go right. This broad forestry track, which is a bridleway, descends to Park House, where you continue straight on for Kinlet North Mountain Bike Area. Go over the ford at speed and then turn sharp left back along a forestry track to regain the bridleway.

Follow the forestry track west until you see the bridleway post, where you go right and up the steep hill on a single track, which can be soft in wet, but a fun little hill climb in the dry. At the top you pass through some very pleasant woodland where, on a quiet day, you may be lucky to see fallow deer. Eventually, after crossing over a forestry road, the track arrives at a T-junction, where you go right.

Descend steeply, cross over a stream and up the hill the other side. The bridleway eventually does a left turn into the wood and, on joining another track, bears left, following the waymarker. At a fork bear right, and climb up into the dark, dark woods, until you come out onto the clearing above the Elan Valley Pipeline. Bear right and up hill to a forestry road, where you go left and then almost immediately fork right. Follow this excellent track down to the B4194 road.

At the road go right and after a short distance you will see a sign on the left indicating Forestry Commission Buttonoak. Take the track into the North Kinlet area and almost immediately bear left, past a barrier, and along a wide grassy track. After climbing out of a little dip you come to some gates, which is the boundary of a very hush-hush top security establishment. Go right and along an excellent little single track which winds its way through the thick wood, but watch out for tree roots. Soon you come to a clearing and the track does a left turn. This is a beautiful, quiet area that is much frequented by mountain bikers. The track follows around the western side of the clearing and descends to a main forestry track. Go right here and follow alongside a small valley and stream, descending a little all the time. Eventually the track veers left and starts to climb again. After about a kilometre of gentle climbing you branch right and descend a forestry road. Shortly, you branch right again onto a smaller track, and then right again. This takes you down to a bridge over a little stream, and then up to a stone road, which is actually a bridleway. Go left here and follow this up to a lane, where the route goes left.

Follow the lane down to the **B4194** at **Buttonbridge**, where you go right. After about 500m fork left for Sturt Common. Enjoy a restful amble along the quiet country lane, with fine views of the Clee Hills to the west. The lane enters the woods, bends left, then just as it bends right you will see a lane straight ahead for Winwoods. A short distance further on is a lane leading off left for Kingswood.

Although both of these lanes connect to a dead-end RUPP, they are not accepted as rights of way. Our route continues down the road, through the private woods of Sturt Common. Eventually the road descends and doubles back to the left, then after about 500m go left at a junction. Follow this twisty lane past cottages until you arrive at a right-hand bend. Ahead (left) is a track signed 'Rudd's Bridge", with a bridleway sign opposite. Follow this track downhill into the woods. Ford a small stream (or use a little bridge) and then cross over Dowles Brook via a larger (broken!) bridge, and up to a forestry track, where you go right.

Follow the bridleway, which can be a little soggy in places, until it brings you back to the forestry road you started out on and the ford. Go right here and climb back up to the junction at Park House. At this point you could return to the start the way you came, or alternatively you could go left along the disused railway track which heads for Bewdley and is used as a Family Bike Route. Enjoy an easy ride along the disused railway track for about a kilometre, until you reach a signpost. Go right for Callow Hill Visitors Centre and immediately fork left. The track follows alongside a little valley, climbing steadily all the time. Go left at a junction where it is signed Visitors Centre and follow the waymarkers back to the start of the route. Enjoy a nice cup of tea at the visitors centre!

Ford over Dowles Brook

Severn Valley

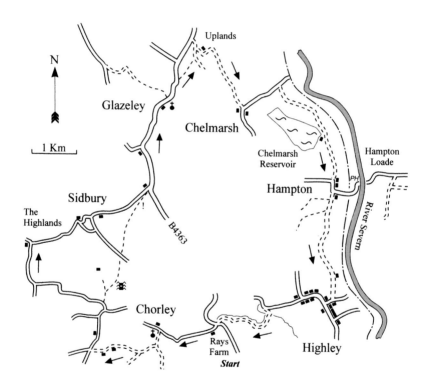

Severn Valley

Route Summary
Rays Farm, High Green, Upper Harcourt, Chorley, Sidbury, Deuxhill, Glazeley, Uplands, Chelmarsh, Hampton, Highley, Rays Farm.

Details
Grade – Moderate
Time – 3 hrs
Distance –   27km
   off road – 14km
   on road – 13km
Terrain – Some hills
Surface – Excellent gravel tracks with some soft, but tricky, bridleways
Start Grid Reference – SO 714 832
Maps – Wyre Forest & Kidderminster E 218, Kidderminster & Wyre Forest area L138.

Introduction
This route is set in the gentle rolling countryside to the west of the Severn Valley, just to the south of Bridgenorth. Although the area is now composed mainly of mixed farming with remnants of the ancient Wyre Forest, it is hard to imagine that in the recent past the south of the area was a busy mining community. The village of Highly has a long industrial heritage, mining in the area having continued up until the late 1960's. The route starts to the west of Highly at Rays Farm, an ideal place to take the kids to see the animals, but also an excellent place to park, and have refreshments at the end of the ride! This is also the start of the Jack Mytton Way, a long distance bridleway, but more of that later.

The route is predominantly one of two halves. Although the first half is mostly on road, it is along very quiet country lanes with little traffic. There is an opportunity for some off-road from near Chorley to Deuxhill, but biker beware, there are some problems! The really fun part of the route is on the return from Glazely, which follows the Jack Mytton Way, along some excellent tracks with fine views of the Severn Valley. After passing Chelmarsh Reservoir we arrive at Hampton and, although not strictly on the route, this is an opportunity to pop down the hill to see the foot-ferry across the Severn at Hampton Loade, and have a drink whilst admiring the view. The route continues via excellent tracks to Highley, with a fun ride through the woods to finish off with.

Route Description

Park at Rays Farm, resisting the temptation to fester in the café (you can do that at the end) and head west along the lane, climbing steadily. Where the lane enters woods at High Green you will see a sign for a caravan site on the left, by the Baptist Chapel. Take this lane and bear right (straight on) down a track by the side of the caravan park. Descend through woods on an excellent track, over a stream via a little bridge, and up towards a new house in the woods. Bear right at the fork, eventually leaving the woods, and then take first right for Harcourt. This area of little hills is beautiful and quiet on a fine summer day. Climb steadily past Lower then Upper Harcourt to arrive at a lane.

There now follows a section along quiet, pretty country lanes that, whilst not being off-road, is still a pleasure to ride. You will see little traffic on these lanes, so enjoy the views. At the lane go right for **Chorley** and enjoy a fast descent, over a stream and up to a junction. Go right here and then sharp left along a narrow lane. Those who have studied the maps carefully will note that there is a bridle-way which starts at a lane on the right, and which runs north for about 2·5 km. If you fancy your chances, have a try, but be aware that the going is difficult! Our route continues along the pretty lane, which can be mucky enough in places, and up to a T-junction. Go right here and then first right at **The Highlands** farm. Follow the lane into **Sidbury**, going left for Bridgenorth, then right. The fast lane takes you down to Horsford on the **B4363**.

Go left here and pick up speed for the climb up to Deuxhill. This may not be the most fun section, but at least it's fast, and soon you 'll descend past **Glazeley** and over Borle Brook. As the road starts to bear left and climb you will see a bridleway on your right. Go through the gate and follow this up the right-hand edge of a field on a good grassy track. Cross over the farm drive at the top and continue along the left-hand edge of the field to arrive at another track. Go left here and follow the little lane around the back of some cottages to arrive at a splendid white house called **Uplands**. Follow the bridleway around the back of the house and past some barns. The bridleway heads downhill slightly and then bears right. You are now on the Jack Mytton Way, with fine views of the Severn Valley on your left.

After a kilometre or so the farm track goes left, but you continue straight on where there is a waymarker. The grassy lane eventually brings you out at some houses and onto the road at **Chelmarsh**. The Jack Mytton Way at this point actually crosses over and takes a back lane down past the Chelmarsh reservoir, and then crosses some grassy fields. As this can be slightly difficult going for bikes, we will go left at the road and down hill. After less than a kilometre we arrive at Crateford and a bridleway on the right, sign-posted 'Dinney Farm B&B'. Follow this gravel track, but where it bears right for the farm, you continue straight on. If you are lucky you might even see a steam loco on the Severn Valley railway at this point! Eventually the gravel track bears left towards a farm, but you go right and through a small bridle gate. The grassy track climbs steadily up to-wards some trees, where you re-join the Jack Mytton Way. This is also a nice spot for a quick snack, as there are good views of the reservoir at this point.

There now follows something of a challenge. Continue straight on through the gate and downhill past the sailing club. The broad grassy lane becomes quite steep, and can also be a little(!) chopped up by horses. This can be as challenging a task as any rocky descent, but with the added advantage of only a face full of mud and a soft landing, if you don't make it! At the bottom you cross over a stream and then go up to a private drive. Continue straight on along the bridleway until you come to a public road. Carry on through the village of **Hampton**, and where the road bears left you continue straight on, at a bridleway sign. Alternatively, at this point you could take a short detour down the lane to Hampton Loade on the river Severn, to see the foot ferry and, more importantly, to enjoy refreshments at the Unicorn Inn. Unfortunately, this means a bit of a climb back up to the route, but it is well worth it.

Continue along the bridleway, through three gates, past some barns and then along a grassy, tree-lined lane. The bridleway runs along the top of fields on a good track, with excellent views of the Severn Valley to the left, and then, after a gate, joins a farm track. Following another gate, bear left and down to the bottom corner of the field, but watch out for the bog in the middle! (Unfortunately, the bridleway does not follow the track along the top and then down the side of the field to avoid the bog, so we can't go that way). Exit the field via a small bridle gate and continue along the right-hand edge of the field, then around the back of some barns. The bridleway then passes through a hole in the wall (I kid you not!) and along a fenced off grassy track by the side of an interesting black and white cottage. After joining a farm drive, you continue on for WoodCott, where you go right and up into the village of **Highley**.

At the B4555 in Highley go right and follow the road around, forking left along a lane where it is signed 'New England Billingsley via ford'. Follow the lane downhill into woods, but just after the lane bears right you will see a sign for the Jack Mytton Way on your left – easy to miss, so don't get too carried away with the speed, unless of course you want to have fun at the ford. Follow the Jack Mytton Way down a tricky and steep little section through the woods, to arrive at the Donkey Bridge. Go over this, bear left then right, and up to a bigger track. This track, which is the route of an old railway line, follows a small brook on your right. If you look out you will see much evidence of the long-dead mining activity that used to be hereabouts. Eventually, the track brings you out to a road, where you go right then immediately left and back to Rays Farm.

Bridge near Lower Chorley

Wenlock Edge

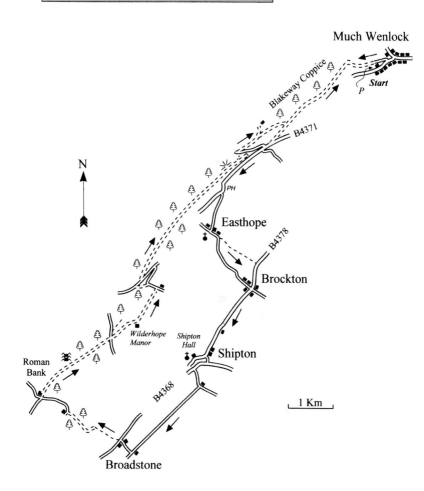

Much Wenlock

Start

P

Blakeway Coppice

B4371

N

PH

Easthope

B4378

Brockton

Wilderhope Manor

Shipton Hall

Shipton

Roman Bank

B4368

1 Km

Broadstone

Wenlock Edge

Route Summary
Much Wenlock, Blakeway Coppice, Wenlock Edge Inn, Brockton, Shipton, Broadstone, Coats Wood, Wilderhope Manor, Disused railway track, Blakeway Coppice, Much Wenlock.

Details
Grade – Very Difficult
Time – 4 Hrs
Distance – 36 km
    off road – 24 km
    on road – 12 km
Terrain – Hilly
Surface – Firm gravel through to very soft woodland tracks
Start Grid Reference – SO 613 997
Maps – Kidderminster & Wyre Forest area, L138

Introduction
To the west of Bridgenorth lies an escarpment of limestone that runs roughly north-east south-west for over fifteen miles. This edge is important geologically and economically speaking, and over 400 million years ago the area was a warm sea full of coral reefs and swarming with life. Today the rock, which has been thrust up and eroded, forms a long thin edge, which rises gently on the east, but drops away steeply to the west. Much of the edge is shrouded in trees, but where there is clearing, fine views to the west of the Caradoc Hills and the Long Mynd can be seen. The area has much history and folklore associated with it, not the least of which is that of Major Smallman of Wilderhope Manor. Apparently, during the Civil War, this gallant fellow, finding himself being chased by parliamentarians, tried to make his escape on horse. Unfortunately, trapped by

the cliff face of the Edge and with his enemy behind, he made a last desperate attempt for freedom and forced the horse to leap. Needless to say, the horse died, but the Major survived to fight another day. Don't be attempted to try this on your bike. Horses are a little softer than bikes and it won't do anything for your suspension!

A slight complication of this route is that it really wants to be a linear route. As I prefer my days out to be circular if possible, the route does contain a middle section on road, but this is either a fast downhill or along a very quiet back lane. This also gives an opportunity for an excellent hill climb out of Broadstone back onto the Edge, with off-road tracks and a disused railway line to take us back to Much Wenlock. A final word of caution! The bridleways are much used by horses, particularly around Roman Bank, and the going can be very tough after wet weather.

Route Description

Park at the National Trust Wenlock Edge carpark on the B4371 Church Stretton road. Take the road back into Much Wenlock, for about 100m, and go left up Blakeway Hollow. The status of this road, which soon becomes a track and is the old road over Wenlock Edge, is not entirely clear. There is, however, a proposal to make it a bridleway and an alternative route for the Jack Mytton Way. The excellent track climbs steadily up hill and enters some woods, Blakeway Coppice. Negotiate the motorcycle trap as best you can and continue on reasonably solid track through the woodland. The track rises and falls gently, passing through some wet bits and also under Major's Leap, until eventually you arrive at a fork in the tracks. Go left here and up hill to arrive at a little carpark and the **B4371**.

Go right onto the B4371 and take the road, which follows along the top of Wenlock Edge. Much of the off-road around here is in woods and below the edge, but this excursion onto the road provides an opportunity to enjoy the tremendous views. Just such an opportunity arises after about a kilometre, where there is a lay-by on the right. Stop off here and clamber up the Wenlock limestone, taking in the grand view to the west of The Lawley, Caer Caradoc, Hope Bowdler and beyond that the Long Mynd. After a quick snack, continue along the road, turning left just past the Wenlock Edge Inn (if you can bear to pass it without stopping!) and down hill into Corve Dale. Pass through **Easthope** and on down to the B4378 at Brockton. There is actually a bridleway out of Easthope but, although it has a reasonable climb, the descent along the edge of arable fields is not so good.

At **Brockton** go right, and along the B4378 for about 2 km. As you come into **Shipton** take a left and down to the B4368 where you go right. Almost immediately you go left for Stanton Long and then right and along Rowe Lane. This delightful little back lane follows along the River Corve and parallel to the main road. Eventually you arrive at a junction where you go right for **Broadstone**, and ahead you will see the hill climb that takes you back up onto Wenlock Edge. The lane takes you down and then up to the B4368, which you cross with care. Opposite you will see a bridleway sign and a sunken lane. The true path of the bridleway follows this lane which, although passable at first, soon becomes totally overgrown and indeed blocked at the top. Follow, therefore, the well-defined track to the left that goes up the right-hand side of the field. This excellent track climbs steadily alongside the fields until it joins a lane, which bears off to the left. Follow this grassy lane and then along a track, which continues to climb up alongside pasture land and through woods - the whole area has an almost alpine feel about it. Eventually you arrive at a farm, where you bear right and down a tarmac lane.

Follow the lane, which soon brings you up to a junction with a county road, by Chapel Croft cottage. There now follows a slightly tricky bit, to put it mildly! On your right is a very inviting looking lane, which is in fact a bridleway and is part of the Jack Mytton Way. Unfortunately, the inviting bit lasts only as long as there are cottages, whereupon it dives into Coats Wood and becomes a really interesting challenge! A combination of wet, woods and intensive use by horses will probably give you some idea of the nature of the challenge before you. Put on your wellies and negotiate this section as best you can – there probably can't be anything worse! The bridleway does improve and, after much struggling, you exit the wood and continue along the top of a field to arrive at a gate. Cross over the county road and continue straight on along the drive for **Wilderhope Manor**. Owned by the National Trust this rather grand manor house is now used as a youth hostel. After stopping off to admire the manor, continue on the track around the back. The easy stony track eventually does a left turn and takes you towards the woods on Wenlock Edge. Where the road bears right, you go left and down a steep rocky track into the woods. Follow the track down to the road (there is a cut through half way down on the right for the Jack Mytton Way, but it is usually a real quagmire), and go right.

Follow the road up hill for a short distance and re-join the JMW by going left and over the motorcycle trap. Enjoy a fun descent through the wood and down to the disused railway line, where you go right. This next section is the dead opposite of that through Coats Wood. The track is solid, straight and fast, unless that is, you want to stop off to admire the woodland flora and fauna. Continue straight on at the motorcycle traps over the bridge, until you eventually arrive at a junction of tracks. Do not be tempted to go straight on here, as you will eventually come to a tunnel, which is blocked. Go left through a gate where there is a JMW sign and descend to a road. Cross over and continue along a farm track. After a few hundred metres you will see that the JMW bears off to the right, over a motorcycle trap, and up into the woods. Climb steeply through the woods to eventually join the track that you started out on. Follow the roller-coaster track back through Blakeway Coppice and down Blakeway Hollow, to arrive back at the start of the route in Much Wenlock.

Blakeway Coppice

Hope Bowdler

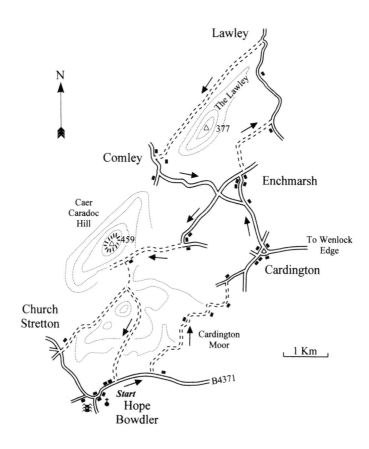

Hope Bowdler

Route Summary
Hope Bowdler, Cardington Moor, Cardington, Enchmarsh, Hoar Edge, The Lawley, Willstone, Hope Bowdler Hill.

Details
Grade – Moderate (tricky sections)
Time – 2 1/2 hrs
Distance –   20 km
   off road – 11 km
   on road –   9 km
Terrain – Hilly
Surface – Grass and stony tracks
Start Grid Reference – SO 478927
Maps – Ludlow, Wenlock Edge & surrounding area, L137.

Introduction
This varied and interesting little route is based around the Caer Caradoc Hills to the east of the Long Mynd. Seen from the latter, this curious chain of hills presents a striking profile, having more in common with the Welsh hills to the west than the lower land of the Midlands to the east. The Caradoc Hills consist of The Lawley, a sort of smaller but steeper sided version of the Long Mynd, Caer Caradoc, Helmeth, Hazler, Ragleth and Hope Bowdler Hills. Although paths cross these hills, many of them are unfortunately footpaths, and therefore a no-go area for mountain bikes. It is possible, however, by linking small country lanes and bridleways together to produce an interesting route that gives something of the flavour of the area. Although most of the route is straightforward there are some steep and rocky sections which present a something of a test of skill.

Route Description

The route starts on the B4371 from Church Stretton to Much Wenlock, where there are a couple of parking places just past the village of Hope Bowdler. Go east along the road until you see Woodgate Cottage on your left. The bridleway, according to the map, starts at the beginning of the drive and bears left to a gate, which leads onto a lane. Most people, however, seem to take the lane from the road just before the drive, even though it is not strictly a right of way. Climb steadily up the stony track, which levels off and bears right. After a gate the track descends steeply to a stream, with lots of loose scree and boulders to test your nerve and skill, and then climbs up equally steeply the other side. After a cattle grid the terrain eases and the track contours around the hill to Middle Hill Farm. Descend past the farm and hairpin right and climb steadily back up. Shortly, the track does a sharp left, becoming concrete which then gives way to tarmac and descends past farms to arrive at a road, where we go left for **Cardington**.

Very soon you arrive at the village but, just as you enter, look out for the rather interesting Brook House on your left, which has a splendid half-timbered entrance and a plaque with the date, 1574 RO over the door. Follow the main road through the village, or make a detour right by St Jame's Church and The Royal Oak pub, until you come to a T-junction, where you turn left. Soon, fork left for Leebotwood and follow the lane out of the village. After about 1/2 km the road bears left, but you fork right and continue climbing up a narrow lane which takes you to the little hamlet of **Enchmarsh**. Fortunately, this is a quiet little lane, so it's quite permissible to get off and push if you need to! Follow the lane through Enchmarsh to arrive at a T-junction. Go right and then very soon, left up a gravel track.

The track climbs gently and then bears right to reveal an impressive view of The Lawley, a long steep sided hill. The track descends

Enjoying a descent

steadily along Hoar Edge, with several boulders and rocks to provide sport, and eventually reaches a road, where you go left and down the hill. Follow the road across the valley towards **The Lawley**, where it does a right turn, descends and bears left around the foot of the hill.

Just as the road does a hairpin right you will see a track on the left, which is a bridleway. Follow this good track past The Well House and along the base of the hill. This delightful track provides a excellent view of the Long Mynd and later on, an impressive view of Caer Caradoc Hill. Apart from a few short sections where it can become rutted, the track is usually in excellent condition. Eventually you reach a gate where you take the right-hand track down to the road. Go left and keep left at a fork, climbing steadily up past Broadstone to a junction near **Enchmarsh**. Turn right, continue to climb up Folly Bank and then descend into Willstone.

As the road does a sharp left in Willstone, turn right up a broad dirt track, signposted '**Caer Caradoc Hill**'. The track climbs steeply along the southern flank of the hill and, just past the remains of Cwms Cottage and a copse, there is a bridleway on the left. This initially ill-defined track contours around the eastern flank of a hillock and then, on a better track, climbs up to a bridle gate. After passing through this, bear left along a grassy track, which starts to climb up Hope Bowdler Hill. Although it is possible to ride at first, the track soon becomes too steep and it is better to dismount rather that churn up the turf and cause irreparable damage (to both you and the ground!). After a short push the terrain eases off and you descend the main broad grassy track with splendid views all around. Eventually, the track becomes steeper and, after passing through a gate, continues down to the road and back to the start. A very pleasant, interesting little route.

One way of getting up Hope Bowdler Hill

Long Mynd - 1

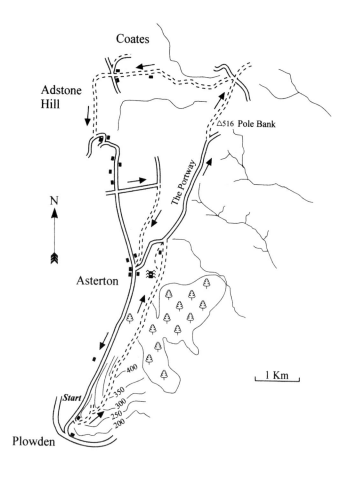

Long Mynd - the quiet way

Route Summary
Plowden, The Port Way, Pole Bank, Coates, Adstone Hill, Prolley
Moor, Asterton, Plowden.

Details
Grade – Difficult
Time – 3 hrs
Distance – 23 km
    off road – 13 km
    on road – 10 km
Terrain – A big hill!
Surface – Moorland tracks, grassy and rocky
Start Grid Reference – SO 384878
Maps – Ludlow, Wenlock Edge & surrounding area, L137.

Introduction
The Long Mynd is justifiably popular with visitors and has been
so since Victorian times. The hill runs approximately north south
and presents a different impression, depending upon your viewpoint.
As one approaches along the main A49 from Shrewsbury, the hill
takes on the appearance of a rather low raised mass of moorland,
outshone by the more impressive Caer Caradoc Hills to the east.
Not until the hill is approached more closely, via the Strettons, does
the broken nature of the eastern side become more apparent. Here,
rivers and waterfalls thread the deep hollows that cut the eastern
flank of the hill. It is easy to see why the Victorians found Carding
Mill Valley so fascinating, and it is still a popular tourist spot today.
The western flank presents an altogether more different aspect. Here
the hill appears long, smooth and steep sided, and has a more
remote feel. The villages on this side of the hill are quiet, unspoilt,
and the lanes almost deserted to the point of being disused.

The route starts on the western side of the hill near the hamlet of Plowden and takes the excellent track from the south, which climbs up onto the Mynd. A short section on road is followed by the final climb to the top at The Pole at 516m where, on a good day, the views can be truly splendid. A fast and fun descent to Coates, followed by a combination of tracks and lanes, returns us to the start. This is an opportunity to see a quieter aspect of the very popular Long Mynd.

Route Description

Park the car somewhere along the road between Asterton and Plowden, and head south on the delightful little lane towards Plowden. Just after passing some cottages on the left you arrive at a cattle grid where you bear left through a bridle gate. This is marked with a bridleway marker and also a little badge (with a galloping horse) informing you that you are on the Jack Mytton Way. This also happens to be the start of the Portway that stretches from end to end of the Long Mynd. Gird up your loins, as the hard part is about to start! The track bears left and then climbs steeply up the hill, to arrive at an enclosure with a couple of gates. Almost immediately you will see that the view to the west and south begins to open up. This is just as well as you will probably need to stop and admire it on several occasions during the climb. Follow the bridleway markers through the gates and on up hill along a well-defined track. After passing through another gate, bear slightly left and continue on a less well-defined track to arrive at gate in the boundary on your left. The track improves and shortly the gradient eases off to reveal the panorama of the Long Mynd stretching out before you to the north. All the effort of the hill climb now seems worthwhile as you gently climb The Mynd, following a green track with heather and bracken on either side. If you are lucky you might even spy a Buzzard or two. After a while you will see a notice on your right informing you the bridleway that you are on is about to cross an airfield, and that you are to watch out for gliders! This might cause some trepidation were it not for the fact that 100m further on is another notice which invites you to take a permissive path around the edge of the airfield. As this provides excellent views of the western side of the Mynd, and is also a great deal safer than having a confrontation with a glider or its towing cable, there isn't really much of a contest. Take the Starboardway, as the track is called, left and follow the little white posts. Eventually the track passes behind the gliding club buildings and to a road.

Continue north along the road, following the route of the old **Portway**. At weekends this small road can get a little busy, particularly with sightseers enjoying the steep ride over the Mynd and also watching gliders, hang-gliders and even parapenters taking advantage of the prevailing south-westerly breeze. Fortunately, although this is likely to be the busiest part of the route, the views are ample compensation. After a couple of kilometres, just past an enclosure of trees, you will see a track and bridleway marker on the left. Jack Mytton has been this way as well! This good track rises up gently to the summit of The Pole, the highest point on the Long Mynd at 1696 feet. Take a rest at the trig point and enjoy the view with the aid of the orientation plate. Apparently, on a clear day, it is even possible to see Snowdon and Cader Idris from this vantage point. At any rate, the views of the Caradoc Hills to the east and the Stiperstones and Wales to the west are spectacular. Suitably refreshed, we now begin a superb descent. Continue along the track, over a little rise and down to the road.

The route goes left, along the road for a short distance, and then bears left and down a track. This pleasant county road, which is no more than a stony track, provides an exciting roller-coaster descent. Eventually you arrive at a gate, after which the well-defined track continues alongside trees, through a couple more gates and down the left-hand side of fields. To your left you now have an excellent view of the wide expanse of the Long Mynd and you might find it hard to believe that you have just biked over this not inconsiderable hill. The track descends into the little hamlet of **Coates**.

Here you have a choice of routes for the return to Plowden. One possibility is to go left at Coates, through a gate and along the county road, which is little more than a track, to **Medlicott**. From there you can follow the road and then the track along the base of the Long Mynd to **Asterton** and finally, Plowden. Our route, however, bears right past some cottages and over a cattle grid and then immediately left and up to a gate. Continue on through this up the left-hand side of a field on a track that is in fact a county road. At the top the track bears left through a couple of gates and then slowly climbs Adstone Hill, little more than a mound in comparison to the Long Mynd. Soon you reach the top and then descend to a gate. The old grassy track continues between lines of trees and after a sweeping descent you arrive at a lane.

Follow the gated lane left and down through Adstone. After a sharp left you descend, (don't go too fast, there's a gate at the bottom!) pass by a couple of farms, eventually reaching a crossroads. Straight on will lead to Asterton, but we go left and up hill for Medlicott. The road climbs gently towards the Mynd and, at such a late stage in the route may seem a little hard on the legs. The benefits of this last little effort are soon revealed however, as, at the top of the road there is a T-junction. A right turn here takes you along a lane, past a farm, through a couple of gates and along a county 'road'. This delightful old track winds its way along the foot of the Long Mynd. Enclosed by trees, it sometimes thinks it's a stream, but rarely becomes too boggy, due to the underlying rock. After going through a gate and on to more open ground, the track descends to Asterton. A left turn in the hamlet will then take you along the road and back to Plowden and the start of the route.

The quiet road to Plowden

Long Mynd - 2

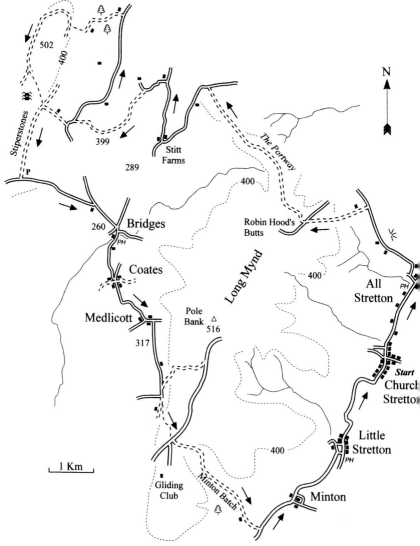

502
400
Stiperstones
P
399
289
Stitt Farms
The Porway
N
260
Bridges
PH
Robin Hood's Butts
400
400
Coates
Long Mynd
All Stretton
PH
Medlicott
Pole Bank △ 516
317
Start
Church Stretton
Little Stretton
PH
400
1 Km
Gliding Club
Minton Batch
Minton

Long Mynd and the Stiperstones

Route Summary
Church Stretton, All Stretton, Plush Hill, The Portway,
Thresholds, Stitt Farms, Leasowes Farms, Brook Coppice,
Stiperstones, Bridges, Coates, Medlicott, Long Mynd, Minton
Batch, Minton, Little Stretton, Church Stretton.

Details
Grade – Very Difficult
Time – 4 hrs
Distance –   42 km
     off road – 22km
     on road – 20km
Terrain – Lots of hills
Surface – Excellent firm gravel tracks and disused lanes
Start Grid Reference – SO 453 938
Maps – Ludlow and Wenlock Edge & surrounding area L137
          Shrewsbury & surrounding area L126

Introduction
This is perhaps the most challenging route in the book and, crossing open moorland several times as it does, is not to be taken lightly. Although the Long Mynd and the Stiperstones can hardly be considered to be mountains, they are, none the less, not kind of place to be caught out in bad weather. However, on a kind day, the views from the top of the Mynd and the Stiperstones are hard to beat. The route starts in the hustle and bustle of Church Stretton and after a stiff climb, you are rewarded with splendid views of Caer Caradoc and The Lawley to the east. Further climbing takes us over the Long Mynd to The Portway, an ancient track that runs the length of the Mynd, and was probably a trade route as far back as Bronze age

times. A combination of tracks and lanes takes us ever closer to The Stiperstones, a wild and rocky moorland, where the wind never seems to cease. There are many associations with the devil and evil doings here, and one can't help but feel slightly uncomfortable when crossing the moor! Fortunately, the Devil's Chair, a curious shaped outcrop is not on the bridleway that traverses the moor, but watch out for witches and 'Wild Edric'! A fast descent with splendid views ahead, followed by more tracks and little lanes, brings us back to the Long Mynd. A final steep climb back over the hill is rewarded with a sublime descent of Minton Batch, which leaves the biker with a contented glow of well being for the final run back into Church Stretton.

Route Description

Start in the centre of Church Stretton and head north along the B4370 towards All Stretton. Soon you arrive at the village, where you go left and up Castle Hill. Climb the steep lane to the top of Plush Hill, where stupendous views to the north-east of the Shrewsbury plain open up before you. Follow the county road until you arrive at a junction just before a cattle grid. Go left here and follow the wide gravel track, which is a bridleway, along the edge of open moorland and up hill. Eventually the track levels off and you come to a county road. Cross over this and continue along a gravel track. Although this ancient track, The Portway, is part designated footpath, bridleway and indeed has no status at all, the whole route is used as a bridleway. Follow the track, which takes you down over a stream and up to a gate. The route continues along a grassy track, through some gates, and above Hawkham Hollow. You then begin to descend, with a fine view of the Stiperstones to the left, and arrive at a gate (white arrow). Continue on with the field boundary now on the left, to arrive at a gate by a barn, with grand views all around. The route continues along a more solid track and eventually brings you to the county road.

Turn left at the county road and enjoy a fun descent to arrive at a junction by Stitt Farms. Go right here for Pulver Batch and follow the road to Leasowes Farms. Go left and follow the little lane down and up towards Leasowes Bank Farm. Where the road bears right for the farm you go left, through a gate and along a grassy track which follows the field boundary and a line of trees. The old road climbs gently, passes through a couple of gates, and then levels off. This section provides absolutely tremendous views of the Stiperstones on your right. After a pleasant little downhill the track arrives at a county road.

Go right and enjoy a fun and fast descent past Gatten Lodge. After a little over 2 km on road you will see a lane on the left for Brook Vessons. Take this, past the farm and some barns, and up a farm track towards Brook Coppice. Enter the wood via a gate and follow the track where it bears left, which eventually takes you to the other side. Exit via a gate and continue, on good solid track, through two more gates and past a house in an idyllic location. The track continues uphill and to the right, to arrive at a bridlegate. Follow the sunken track up into the woods, bearing round to the right. The ill-defined track generally climbs uphill, through a wooded area, and to a gate on the boundary of the Stiperstones Nature Reserve.

Go through this gate and right. Follow the track, which climbs gently and takes you around the northern end of the Stiperstones ridge. Heather and gorse abound, and there are splendid views to the north. After passing through two gates you come to a bridleway junction, where you go left and up the hill. Bear left again where the tracks divide and after some gentle climbing you arrive at the top of the broad ridge. Stop off for a quick snack, enjoy the view, then continue straight on down to a gate. Continue downhill to a farm track, where you go right, and then right again where it is signed the Kennels Carpark. Follow the track up to a gate at the edge of some woods, then up and along the eastern side of the Stiperstones. Eventually the track brings you out at the carpark and the county road.

At the road go left and, after many cattle grids and a blistering descent, you eventually come to a T-junction. Go left here, then immediately right and into Bridges, then right again. Stop off for a quick pint at the pub (but not too much, there is a way to go yet) and then continue up the lane through Overs and on to Coates. Go through the farm at Coates and straight on for Medlicott. The little used lane drops down into a valley, then climbs up to the hamlet of Medlicott, and then bears right for Prolley Moor. Follow the lane along below the Long Mynd and, where the road does a sharp right, you continue straight on at the 'No Through Road' sign.

About 100m along the lane there is a bridleway on the left. This can be a bit tricky to begin with, but it soon opens out and improves. (If the weather has been wet an alternative route to the top of the Mynd could be taken by following the track up Stanbatch, which is a UCR.) This steep and punishing track climbs directly to the top of the Long Mynd, bringing you out at the road near the entrance to the gliding club. Cross straight over the road and across open moor, looking for an initially ill-defined track. Soon the track becomes evident and the descent of Minton Batch begins. Words cannot describe the joy of this descent. The narrow track weaves its way down the side of the stream, alternately dipping into bogs and leaping over rocks, never too technical, but just enough to be pure fun. The moorland scenery around is more reminiscent of further north, perhaps Yorkshire, and is MTB heaven! Eventually the track arrives at a farm (Best Kept Farm Award 1999!) and joins the main farm track, which takes you down to a lane.

At the lane go left for Minton and as you come into the hamlet, bear left for Little Stretton. Zip down the hill and into the village, where you go left and then left again onto the B4370. Follow the road, which soon takes you back to Church Stretton and the start of the route.

A very satisfying day out!

The Stiperstones in the far distance from the UCR near Leasowes

Ludlow

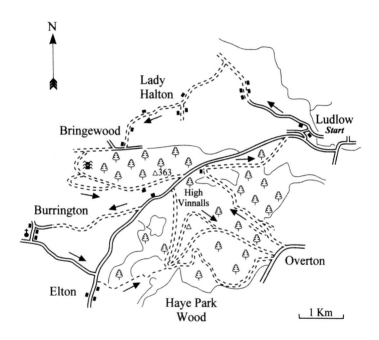

N

Lady
Halton

Bringewood

Ludlow
Start

△363

High
Vinnalls

Burrington

Overton

Elton

Haye Park
Wood

1 Km

Ludlow

Route Summary
Ludlow, Priors Halton, Lady Halton, Deepwood, Gorsty, Monstay Rough, Burrington, Elton Hall, High Vinnalls, Mary Knoll Valley and House, Upper Evens, Ludlow.

Details
Grade – Very difficult
Time – 3 1/2 hrs
Distance –   31 km
   off road – 24 km
   on road –   7 km
Terrain – Hilly
Surface – Mostly forestry tracks, some field bridleways
Start Grid Reference – SO 507744
Maps – Ludlow, Wenlock Edge & surrounding area, L137

Introduction
Ludlow is reputed to be one of the most charming country towns in England. The well-preserved 900 year old castle looks particularly grand when seen from Whitcliffe across the River Teme, and this is where our route starts. The extensive woods to the west of Ludlow form part of the Forestry Commission Mortimer Forest, an area well known to local mountain bike enthusiasts, as well as walkers. The Commission has created waymarked walks of varying difficulty, but fortunately for us, they also have an enlightened attitude towards mountain bikers! At the time of going to print, mountain bikers were allowed to bike almost anywhere, provided they kept clear of the waymarked walks, kept their speed down and respected other users of the forest. With such freedom to roam it is possible to create any number of routes, but it is probably a good idea to call at

the Whitcliffe visitors centre to see if there are any temporary restrictions in force. One problem with all forestry, however, is that it can be very easy to get lost! Also, forestry routes can get a little monotonous at times. With this route, I have tried to incorporate a little variety by including sections outside the forest. The route warms up with an easy excursion north via the Haltons, followed by a stiff climb up into Bringewood, with superb views as a reward. An easy run down into Burrington and across to Elton, is followed by more climbing and then a swift descent into Haye Park. From there the bridleway up Mary Knoll Valley is taken, with more fine views, and then back to Ludlow.

Route Description

Leave Ludlow via the Dinham Bridge and just as the lane starts to climb, go right and straight ahead, where it is signed for the Cliff Hotel. Unfortunately, it's too soon to stop for a drink, so continue along the lane for Priors Halton. This little lane provides an excellent view of the forest on your left, a glimpse of things to come. At the farm, continue straight on where it is signed 'Private - No Through Road' - this is in fact a bridleway. After going past a gate you enter the Oakly Park estate. About 300m along the tree-lined drive you will see another tarmac track on the left. Follow this through **Lady Halton**, where it becomes a gravel track, and on up towards the forest. Eventually the track arrives at a lane at a Brick House, where you go right. After 300m the lane bears to the right, but you continue straight on, into Deep Wood.

Follow along the edge of the wood, ignoring the first major left, until after about 1/2 km, just past a little stream, fork left and up a steep grassy track. Push and pant your way up this testing little climb, to arrive at a rather strange building on your left. This, in fact, was built by the Birmingham Corporation Water Board and is part of the Elan Valley supply, which is of such importance to the folk of Birmingham. Continue on up through the trees, out onto a forestry track, where you go right and up hill. The track zigzags its way up hill and then begins to level out. About 200m after the last bend (look out for the fine view of Downton Castle) do a double-back right. Shortly this brings you to the edge of the Forestry Commission land where you bear left, following the boundary up hill. This is fun biking and as you climb, a superb vista opens out before you. Continue up hill until, at the top (339m), there is a seat. Stop here and have a rest because the view, on a good day, is special! To the west you can see the hills of Wales and the borderlands, whilst south and east is a fine view of the rest of the forest, which we shall shortly be visiting.

Suitably refreshed, continue downhill to join a main forestry track from the left, which is followed down and along the edge of **Bringewood**, eventually reaching Gorsty. At the road, go right and down hill. After a little over a kilometre, just past a house, there is a track on the right. Follow this, through a gate, and on through Monstay Rough. This delightful little track winds its way down through Long Larches (Forestry Commission) until it arrives at **Burrington**, where you go left.

Follow the lane out of the sleepy little hamlet to a T-junction, where the route goes left. A couple of kilometres along this lane you arrive at the Wigmore road where you turn right. Just before **Elton** Hall is a bridleway on the left, with a very curious little sheep-house in the neighbouring field. Follow the bridleway up the left-hand side of the field, bearing right onto a more definite track, and into trees. The track climbs steadily up beside a stream, but is sometimes poorly defined. After a couple of fields and a wood, you come out into a large field. Continue to climb until you see on the right a bridge over the stream and a gate. Go through this (barn on your right) and then follow the track up hill and to the left. Again, the track disappears, but continue straight on until you see a gate on the right, which is the entrance to Brush Wood. This leads onto a track, where you go left and then immediately right and up hill into the wood. This particular track can be a little rutted and soft at times.

Soon you arrive at the top and emerge onto a large forestry track. Go right here and then first left. Climb steadily on an excellent forestry track until you reach the top of **High Vinnalls**. Admire the superb views and have a break, then continue on, bearing right and follow the obvious track downhill to the Haye park carpark.

Go left onto the road and down towards **Overton**. As the road bears right, you go left and along the main track up Mary Knoll Valley. About 100m after the sign telling you that you are in Sunny Dingle Wood, fork right and up the hill past the cottage of the same name. Just past this, the main track does a hairpin right, but you continue straight on along a dirt track. A couple of hundred metres after a pool, the track bears left over the stream, but you carry on along a smaller track. Shortly, you arrive at a gate which advertises that you are entering private woods, the Mary Knoll conservation area, so keep to the track. After another gate, you continue to climb up across a large field used for grazing (good views), and eventually arrive at Mary Knoll House. Go past the house, through a gate into a field, immediately right and through another gate by a barn. Follow the right-hand edge of the field up to another gate and into the woods. Continue along the side of the wood and basically straight ahead, ignoring any tracks to the left or right. After passing the Whitcliffe visitor's centre, the track becomes narrow and quite technical in places. This is impossible to ride up, but the little drop-offs are quite fun on the way down. Make sure you've got your helmet on and take it easy! Too soon, you arrive at the road where you go right. A first left and a hairpin bring you back down to the Dinham Bridge and into Ludlow.

Lower Whitcliffe from Priors Halton

Hopton Castle

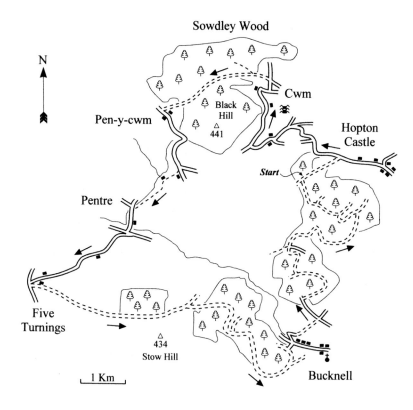

Sowdley Wood

N

Cwm

Pen-y-cwm

Black
Hill
△
441

Hopton
Castle

Start

Pentre

Five
Turnings

△
434
Stow Hill

Bucknell

1 Km

Hopton Castle

Route Summary

Hopton Titterhill, Cwm, Sowdley Wood, Pen-y-cwm, Pentre,
Five Turnings, Stow Hill, Bucknell Wood, Bucknell Hill, Hopton
Titterhill.

Details

Grade – Very Difficult
Time – 4 Hours
Distance – 35 Km
    off road – 22 Km
    on road – 13 Km
Terrain – Very Hilly, wooded
Surface – Mostly forestry tracks and green lanes.
Start Grid Reference – SO 348778
Maps – Ludlow, Wenlock Edge and surrounding area L137.

Introduction

This challenging route is located around the mountain bike trails
at Hopton Castle, situated just eight miles west of Craven Arms and
close to the Shropshire-Hereford border. The Forestry Commission,
with their very enlightened attitude, have devised a number of trails
within Hopton Wood specifically for mountain bikers. The woods
occupy about 860 acres and there are trails to suit all abilities. Trails
are marked with numbered posts and there is an excellent guide
available from the Forestry Commission. For those with a more
adventurous nature, however, this route is presented as an alternative.

The area is characterised by some quite respectable hills, inter-
leaved with little country lanes that have all but fallen into disuse.
Although classified as county maintained roads, it appears that some

of them have seen little maintenance for many a year! This is particularly the case around Llanadevy and Cwm, allowing a very pleasant link between Hopton Titterhill and the Forestry Commission Sowdley Wood. Small roads, followed by a fun bridleway with superb views, bring us to Pentre and then on to Five Turnings. Here we take the bridleway over Stow Hill (difficult in places) and enjoy a relaxing descent though Bucknell Wood, also owned by the Forestry Commission. A stiff little climb up Bucknell Hill returns us to the Hopton Wood bike trails, where we can take any route of our choice, depending on how much energy is left!

Route Description

The route starts at the forestry carpark at Hopton Titterhill. Leave the delights of Hopton Woods behind for later and head back down the track to the road. Turn left here and climb steadily through trees, then fork right for Llanhowell. Soon you arrive at a crossroads on a bend. Straight on takes you to the farm, but the status of the track beyond is in dispute, so we go left and up the hill. The barely maintained lane climbs up through trees, past a farm, to arrive at a T-junction, where you go right. Eventually, this narrow and overgrown lane takes you down past a trout farm at **Cwm** and then uphill again. Take the next left up a very disused road, which is more off-road than on. At the top go left, through a gate and up a grassy track, which is signed as a by-way.

This by-way can be rather overgrown later on in the season, but persevere as at the top is another gate, after which the track gets a little easier. Follow this up the side of the wood and after about 100m, you will see a track, which enters the wood. Here you have a choice. The first option is to continue straight on along the track by the side of the wood. This will shortly bring you to a gate, the other side of which is a section of overgrown track, about 200m or so. Once past this the going gets easier (and prettier) and eventually you join a main forestry track which takes you down to the crossroads near Pen-y-cwm. Alternatively, the second option is to go right, following the narrow track through the wood, dodging tree stumps, low branches and the like. Soon the track opens out and you can then enjoy a relaxing run down through **Sowdley Wood** on the main forestry track. Unfortunately, all good things come to an end and you soon arrive at a road at Woodend, where you continue straight on (left) and up a very steep hill. Eventually you arrive at the same crossroads near **Pen-y-cwm**. The choice is very simple, an easy way down through the wood and then steep climb back up, or fight your way through the gorse along the old county road!

Either way, continue south-east along the road past Pen-y-cwm farm and round the Fiddler's Elbow. Soon there is a junction where the road bears left, but you go right and through a gate just before a barn. Go through a second gate and then follow the obvious track, with fine views, which goes down the hill and eventually arrives at a farm. Turn left here and go down to a gate. On your left you will see two gates. Take the one on the left and follow a steep track up the right-hand side of the field to another gate on the right. A steep and slightly tricky descent then follows, which soon brings you to a cottage. After negotiating a few more gates and enjoying a very pleasant ride alongside a stream, you eventually arrive at a road. Go left here and down to **Pentre**. At the T-junction turn left and then, very soon, sharp right and up the road for 'Five Turnings'.

The road climbs steeply, then more gently and after a while reaches the main road at **Five Turnings**. Double back left past a house, following an excellent track, which is a by-way, up **Stow Hill**. As you climb the track becomes narrower, until you reach a gate. The track continues alongside an arable field and can be difficult, depending on the time of year. Continue through another couple of gates and then along the edge of a wood. The track climbs gently until, at the end of the wood, it starts to descend towards Bucknell Wood. Follow the major Forestry Commission track through the wood, which provides a fun descent and leads to the valley bottom. Continue on the track around the base of the hill, ignoring the track to Bucknell, and then go right at the end of the wood to the road.

On the other side of the road is a footbridge over the River Redlake. Cross this or ford the river and then go left and up a small lane. This leads to a gate by a house and then does a sharp right uphill and past the back of the house. The road becomes a delightful little grassy track with a good view back down to **Bucknell**. Eventually, after passing through some gates, the track leads onto a lane. Turn left here and continue on up hill towards Bucknell Hill. At the top is an entrance to the Hopton Titterhill and Bucknell Hill Forestry Commission woods and bike trails. As the Forestry Commission particularly welcomes mountain bikes here, you can basically go where you like. For those tired after a hard day there is an easy track around the east of Bucknell Hill to a junction above Mereoak Farm. Continue roughly east and then zigzag back over the top of Hopton Titterhill and down to the carpark.

The county maintained road down to Pen-y-cwm

Clun & Bury Ditches

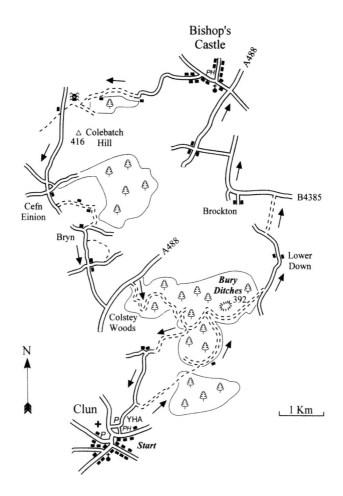

Bishop's
Castle

A488

PH

Colebatch
416 Hill

Cefn
Einion

Brockton

B4385

Bryn

A488

Lower
Down

*Bury
Ditches*
392

Colstey
Woods

N

Clun

P YHA
PH

Start

1 Km

Clun and Bury Ditches

Route Summary
Clun, Radnor Wood, Sunnyhill, Bury Ditches, Lower Down, Colebatch, Bishop's Castle, Woodbatch, Cefn Einion, Bryn, Colstey Woods, Guilden Down, Clun.

Details
Grade – Difficult
Time – 4hrs
Distance –   30km
    off road – 15km
    on road – 15km
Terrain – Hills
Surface – Forestry roads, grassy by-ways and bridleways
Start Grid Reference – SO 303 811
Maps – Ludlow, Wenlock Edge & surrounding area L137.

Introduction
This route starts in the delightful little town of Clun, an excellent centre for exploring the beautiful countryside hereabouts. The whole area is steeped in history, and a visit to Clun Castle is a must. The motte and bailey castle was built by Robert de Say, a Marcher Lord, in about 1140 and stands atop a natural rocky mound, by the side of the River Clun. Later, a more substantial Norman stone castle was built, and the ruins still look very grand today, particularly when viewed from the surrounding hills.

Just to the north-east of Clun is Colstey Woods and Bury Ditches. Forest Enterprise have created a bike route that runs from the main A488 on the west side, to the Bury Ditches carpark on the east, and this is used in the route described. Bikes are not allowed on the impressive iron age earthworks, but do take time to have a look, as the views are quite splendid form the top.

Further north still is the ancient town of Bishop's Castle. Unfortunately, little remains of the original Norman castle built for the Bishop of Hereford, but the little town boasts two museums and many picturesque buildings and traditional shops. There are also six pubs, two breweries and tea and coffee shops. Stop here for too long and you won't get going again!

Route Description

Start at the Community Centre carpark in Clun. Head out of the carpark and left. The lane takes you past the YHA, and where it does a sharp left and starts to climb, you continue straight on along a green lane. This lane bears left and starts to climb up a sunken track, enclosed by trees. The track steepens, but the going is usually reasonable. Eventually, you arrive at a gate and continue straight on up the left-hand side of a couple of fields on a good track. At the top of the hill you enter Radnor Wood via a large gate and then enjoy a steep descent through the woods. Even after wet, this track is usually in good condition, probably because it seems to be little used by horses. Exit the wood via a gate and continue down the right-hand side of a field used for grazing. After going through another large gate, bear left across the field, ford a stream and up to a track with a footpath sign. Go right here, then immediately double back left and up to an old gate, which takes you into the Forestry Commission woods.

Go right at the forestry track and climb up gently around the edge of Steepleknoll woods to arrive at a T-junction. Here you will see that you have joined the Jack Mytton Way and the Bury Ditches bike route. Go right here, following the easy forestry road along the edge of Sunnyhill and below **Bury Ditches**. There are particularly splendid views to the south, looking down to Clunton and across to Sowdley Wood (and the Hopton route). Eventually the track brings you out at the main carpark - time to have a quick snack! If time allows, pop up and have a look at the Bury Ditches earthworks, but lock up the bikes and leave them behind, as they are not allowed on the ancient monument.

At the road, go left and enjoy a kamikaze descent through the hamlet of **Lower Down** (which it is!), but make sure the brakes are in good condition as you need to look out for a by-way on the right. Follow this track, which can be a little wet in places (or even flooded), over the River Kemp via a couple of little bridges, to arrive at a road, the **B4385**.

Take a left turn here and after about a kilometre, another left turn for Colebatch. Soon the lane brings you to the main **A488** at Colebatch, where you go right for **Bishop's Castle**. After about a kilometre, go left for the town, and as the road bears right, continue straight on (left). (Alternatively, you could stop off to sample the delights of the many pubs or the excellent coffee shop at the top of the High Street, before making the return journey). Follow the lane up hill, taking the second left along Woodbatch Road. Soon the tarmac ends and, after a farm, becomes a bridleway. Continue past Middle Woodbatch Farm via a gate, fork left, and up a sunken and beautiful tree-lined track. The going gets steeper, but eventually you exit the woods and arrive at a flimsy wire fence. Although this is the Shropshire Way and a bridleway, some locals do not seem to appreciate that people, bikes and horses have a right of way. Go over the fence and continue up the sunken lane out onto a field. Bear left at the end of the field, then over a stile (the old gate is well and truly tied up!). Continue along the right-hand edge of the field, through another gate and past some barns, out onto a lane.

At the lane go left and enjoy the fine views to the west of Offa's Dyke and Wales beyond. A fast descent brings you to the hamlet of **Cefn Einion**, where you continue straight on. About 100m past the converted Methodist Church you will see a little detour. Strictly speaking, this is not really necessary, but it does add a bit of off-road fun. Take the excellent track left, which climbs up gently past a cottage, then bears right at a house. The fun and at times, rocky descent brings you to a lane, where you go right and up the hill for the hamlet of **Bryn**. Take a left turn for Clun, and follow the lane to the main A488.

At the main road go left and down the hill for about a kilometre, until you see the entrance to **Colstey Woods** on the right. Follow the excellent forestry track, which descends and then climbs again. The track seems to leave the wood for a while and then arrives at a junction, where you go right. As you climb up through the woods you eventually see a sign for Clun pointing back to your right. This is also the Jack Mytton Way, the Shropshire Way and Wild Edric's Way - a lot of strange people have been this way! Follow the track down through the woods, past a pool and eventually join tarmac. After passing through the farms of Guilden Down, the lane descends rapidly and soon you arrive back at the start in Clun.

The bridleway up to Radnor Wood

Clun & Offa's Dyke

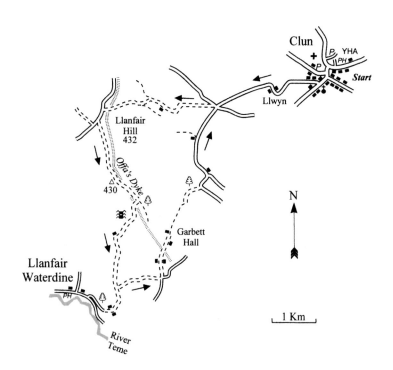

Clun and Offa's Dyke

Route Summary
Clun, Llwyn, Llanfair Hill, Offa's Dyke, Llanfair Waterdine, Garbett Hall, Upper Treverward, Clun.

Details
Grade – Moderate
Time – 2 1/2hrs
Distance – 19km
    off road – 12km
    on road – 7km
Terrain – Hills
Surface – gravel/rocky tracks
Start Grid Reference – SO 300 807
Maps – Ludlow, Wenlock Edge & surrounding area L137

Introduction
This short but hilly route is ideal for those who want a quick insight into what the area has to offer. The route starts in Clun and climbs onto Llanfair Hill via Llwyn. Those who lack the stamina might prefer to park near GR 276 801 so avoiding the initial climb, but then they would miss the fun descent at the end of the day!

The route follows the Jack Mytton Way up onto Llanfair Hill and follows a section of Offa's Dyke for about 2km south. The idea of building an enormous ditch which would stretch from the Dee in the north to the confluence of the Wye and Severn in the south, as a means of securing the land to the west of the Severn, is hard to comprehend, but it worked. This enormous defence apparently brought relative peace and harmony to the area. Today, the Welsh have long since decided that England it is not worth invading any more, and the area is peaceful, punctuated only occasionally by a lone long distance walker or bike rider.

A steep and rocky descent follows the Jack Mytton Way down into Llanfair Waterdine, on the border with Wales (and where there is an excellent pub), then returning by old by-ways and lanes back to the start in Clun. A straightforward route, that offers a taster of this quiet, unspoilt countryside.

Route Description

Start at the Castle carpark (or the Community Centre one if it is full) and follow the A488 south out of Clun, past the church and then right for Springhill. The road climbs steadily up past **Llwyn** (with fine views of the town and castle behind) and eventually arrives at a crossroads. Go right here and then immediately left where there is a bridleway sign. Follow the tarmac farm track to the farm, around the back of some barns, then along a gravel track. In a field, bear left by an oak tree with a Jack Mytton Way sign, and continue up to a gate at the top of the field. The excellent track climbs up a shallow valley, crosses **Offa's Dyke** and finally reaches a lane. Go left here and up the hill.

At the top of the hill you will see a grassy lane on the left and a sign for a by-way and the Offa's Dyke path. Follow this for a short distance to join a gravel track and continue along the right-hand side of the dyke. The riding is easy, with a few gates to negotiate, and splendid views to the east and west. The by-way crosses the dyke, a good place to stop off and have a look at the earthworks, then passes some barns. Turn right by the clump of conifers, through a gate and the dyke again, then descend steeply on a rocky track. After a fast descent you arrive at some barns, where the route bears left. The track descends gently (past a lane on the left), through a farm and finally through woods and down to the narrow lane at **Llanfair Waterdine**. Stop off at the Red Lion Inn for a well-earned drink!

Suitably refreshed, climb back up the way you came, past the farm, and take the lane right that you should have noticed on the way down. Although this is a road, it's in a poor state. Descend to a stream, climb up steeply, and then descend to Selley Cross. Go left here, pass Selley Hall and then Offa's Dyke again, and up to **Garbett Hall**. Go past the barns, through a gate where there is a bridleway sign and follow the rocky track, which climbs uphill. This track passes through a gate and becomes indistinct, but continues straight on to a gate on the far side. Go through this and right to a further gate. The bridleway then continues along the ancient grassy depression and descends to a track, which continues down a delightful valley. After bearing right, you ford a stream, then go up to a gate by a lane.

At the lane go left, past Upper Treverward and start to climb the hill. Eventually you reach the crossroads that you started out on, at the top, and a fast and furious descent takes you back to Clun.

Family day out near Upper Treverward

West Midlands Bike Route

Route Summary
Kinver Edge, Allum Bridge, (Highley), Hampton, Chelmarsh, Glazeley, Eudon George, Meadowley, Shirlett, Much Wenlock, Wenlock Edge, Eaton, Chelmick, Church Stretton, All Stretton, The Portway, Plowden, Lydbury North, Bury Ditches, Clun, Offa's Dyke, Llanfair Waterdine.

Details
Grade – Very very difficult!
Time – Days!
Distance – 120km approx (depending on variation)
    off road – 75km
    on road – 45km
Terrain – Flat bits and hilly bits
Surface – You name it, it's got it!
Start Grid Reference – SO 835 821
Maps – Kidderminster & Wyre Forest area L138, Ludlow, Wenlock Edge & surrounding area L137.

Introduction
The main inspiration for this route was the Jack Mytton Way (JMW), a bridleway route set up by Shropshire County Council in 1993 to celebrate a Shropshire eccentric, Mad Jack Mytton. This completely barking mad character lived in the early part of the nineteenth century, and was famous for his crazy horse rides. As a consequence of these eccentric equestrian pursuits, he spent a vast fortune, ended up in jail, and died there in 1834. He also happened to be a Member of Parliament at one time, but then, bearing in mind his character, that is not so surprising.

The JMW stretches from near Highly in the east of the county, to Llanfair Waterdine in the west. Since the author started researching into off-road routes in the Midlands, it became clear that many of the routes could be linked together to form one super-route, and the idea of the West Midlands Bike Route was born. I have used extensively the JMW, but varied it where I felt that, for example, extra off-road possibilities could be added, or where a better alternative for bikes was available. Although the JMW is a long-distance bridleway, there are some sections that are particularly suited to horses, rather than bikes. A good example of this is the stretch of bridleway through Coats Wood along Wenlock Edge. Unfortunately, no easy alternative exists for this particular section, but occasionally I have been able to take a different route.

Routes are never perfect and can always be improved, and I do not believe this route to be complete. The concept of a route that extends from the very centre of Birmingham out to Wales (Birmingham to the [Welsh] Borders?) has a certain appeal. In theory it ought to be possible to start at Gas Street Basin in the centre of Birmingham and follow the Worcester and Birmingham Canal south to Barnt Green, although you would need to check with British Waterways to see if this were allowed. From there it ought to be possible to link to Kinver via the Lickey and Clent Hills and the bridleways to the south-west of Stourbridge. I have not tried this and I leave this challenge to others who have a greater knowledge of the area.

WMBR - 1

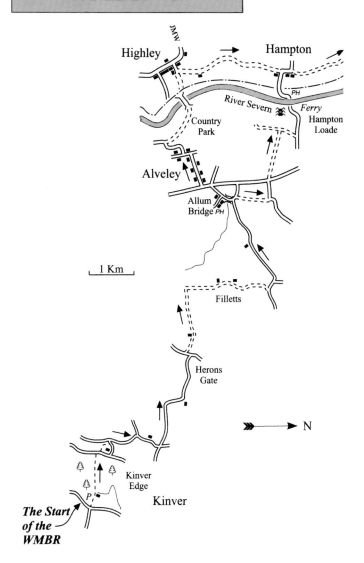

Highley

Hampton

River Severn

Ferry

Hampton Loade

Country Park

Alveley

Allum Bridge *PH*

1 Km

Filletts

Herons Gate

Kinver Edge

Kinver

➤ N

The Start of the WMBR

Kinver Edge to Allum Bridge

The WMBR starts at the carpark on the east side of Kinver Edge at GR 835 821. Follow the bridleway, which climbs steadily up through the woods. Soon the track reaches the top of the edge, at a picnic spot and waymarker. Continue straight on and down (care!) a very steep and narrow track which hairpins through the woods, following the blue waymarkers, until eventually you arrive at the Kingswood carpark on the other side of Kinver Edge.

Go right at the road, then left down a narrow and slightly overgrown lane. The bridleway bears right and arrives at a country lane. Go left here, then right and along Sheepwash Lane. Continue straight on at a junction and left at the crossroads for Romsley. Follow the country lane for a couple of kilometres to a T-junction, where you go left and then first right along a bridleway. This track takes you past Howlet Hall farm and travels west for a kilometre, bears right and continues past Perry House and **Filletts** to arrive at a road. Go left and descend to **Allum Bridge**.

There are now two possibilities for crossing the River Severn, depending upon the time of year.

Hampton Loade variation (April - September, or when the foot ferry is running).

Just before Allum bridge go right and, where the lane bears left, continue straight on up a broad firm track. The by-way climbs the hill, then descends slightly to a road, where you go left and down to the main road.

Cross over the A442 and follow the broad track, which is a byway, until you come to a junction, where you go right. Continue on to a lane, then left and down the hill to the ferry at Hampton Loade. Cross over the **River Severn** and up the hill to Hampton, where you continue north along the JMW and the WMBR.

Alveley variation (all year)

Continue past the Mill Hotel at Allum Bridge and up to the A442. Go left and then right taking you into the large village of **Alveley**. Climb up to a T-junction in the old part of the village and go left.

Take a first right, where it is signed Severn Valley Country Park and, after a left bend, you will notice a bridleway on the right. This crosses reclaimed land and is affected by erosion, therefore, continue on down the lane and enter the park via the drive. Just before the visitor's centre, bear left and go down the main hardcore track, but keep to a reasonable speed. At the bottom you arrive at the old miners bridge over the **River Severn**.

Cross over the Severn and bear right where it says 'Motorcycles Prohibited'. Climb gently up alongside the river to the Country Park halt on the Severn Valley Railway. Cross over the railway (take care!), climb up through the woods, past caravans and a farm to arrive at a junction of tracks just outside Highley. Go right for Woodend to join the JMW.

Byway from Allum Bridges

Top of Kinver Edge – Kingswood

WMBR - 2

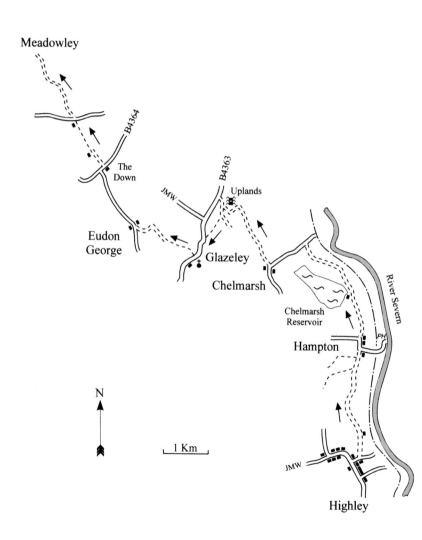

Meadowley

B4364

The
Down

JMW

B4363

Uplands

Eudon
George

Glazeley

Chelmarsh

Chelmarsh
Reservoir

River Severn

PH

Hampton

N

1 Km

JMW

Highley

Highley to Meadowley

Follow the track past Woodcott and, just before Woodend, bear left along a fenced off track, past the cottage and barns, and along the left-hand edge of a field to a bridle gate. Bear left and up hill (through a bit of a bog!) to a track. Continue through a gate and along a track, which passes through a coppice and via gates down to the road in **Hampton**. (The Hampton Loade route variation across the River Severn joins at this point.)

Continue on, but where the road bears left, follow the drive straight on (right). The drive descends and bears left for the sailing club, but you continue on (right), over a stream and up a difficult climb (probably need to get off and carry!). After going through a gate at the top the JMW goes left and through a gate, but we bear right, down a lane to a farm track. Go left here, follow this to a road, then left and up to **Chelmarsh**.

Look out for the JMW signs on the right in the hamlet and follow the lane, which becomes grassy. Eventually you come to a gate and continue straight on along a farm track, bearing left and up to **Uplands**. Follow the bridleway signs around and onto the drive in front of the house and then left (away from the road). The JMW uses country lanes for the next section to The Down, but we will use a bridleway to Eudon George.

Follow the drive around until you see a bridleway on the right. Go down the right-hand edge of a field, over a drive, and continue down the left-hand edge of an arable field to the B4363. Go left, over Glazeley Bridge, and climb up towards **Glazeley** Village.

Opposite the church you will see a bridle gate on the right. Take this across grazing land to a small gate by some trees. Drop down into a wood, over Borle Brook, up past a little cottage, and out into an arable field. Follow along the right-hand edge for a short distance, then cut across the field on a usually well defined, but soft track. At the other side continue on a good solid track which, after a couple of gates, arrives at **Eudon George** Farm.

Go right, following the lane down and then up to the **B4364**, where you go right. Almost immediately go left for Down Farm (now on the JMW again). Climb up the gravel track, bear left and then through a gate on the right. Continue along the left-hand edge of a couple of fields, bearing right at the end of the field. Go through a bridle gate and along the top right-hand edge of fields to arrive at a county road. Cross over and continue on an excellent gravel farm track, which takes you along the top of a broad hill until you reach Meadowley.

Jack Mytton Way near Chelmarsh

WMBR - 3

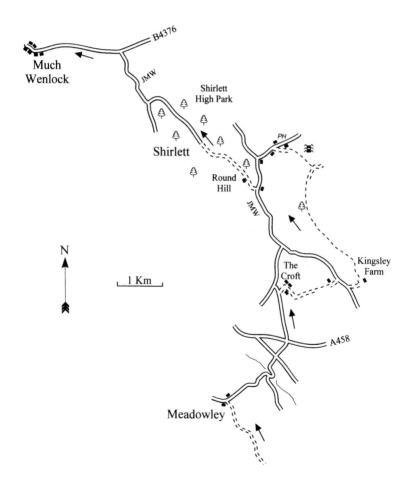

Meadowley to Much Wenlock

At Meadowley go right, down the hill, through pretty woods, over Mor Brook, and up hill to a cross roads. Cross straight over and again at the **A458**, then continue along a country lane. The JMW continues straight on to the bridleway over Round Hill, but the WMBR does a detour first.

At **The Croft** farm go right, down the farm lane, then right again in front of houses. After going through a gate continue along the right-hand edge of a field, through another gate, bear left at the end of a field, descend and cross a short section of arable field. Continue straight on at the double gates, over the stream, and up the left-hand edge of a field towards a farm. Go through a couple of gates and right at the farm drive. Follow this up to the county road, where you go right.

After a few hundred metres go left for **Kingsley Farm**, down the drive, but look out for the re-routed bridleway on the left. This goes around the back of a cottage, along the right-hand edge of a field. Follow this down, then left and along the bottom of the field on reasonable track (Danger! Look out for the badger's set!). Continue through a small gate and along the bottom of another field to a further gate. Cross a couple of arable fields (difficult), along the right-hand edge of the next field on good track, but look out for a small bridle gate hidden by bushes at the end of the field. Continue along the right-hand edge of a couple of fields, through a gate on the right, then along the left-hand edge of the next field. Go past a wood, through a gate and along a fenced off track. Cross an arable field on good track, bear right down to a gate and onto a gravel track. Bear left and up Stocking Lane.

Just before this gravel track starts to climb you will see a narrow tree-lined lane on the left (hidden). Follow this (can be soft and overgrown), which eventually opens out and improves, and takes you down to a lane.

Go left at the lane, bear left again then right, where it is signed Round Hill Farm and rejoin the JMW. The gravel track bears right and enters a steep, narrow tree-lined lane (difficult in places), climbing up and over **Round Hill**. Eventually it joins a part-tarmac lane, which takes you up through the woods (very pleasant riding). Go right at the T-junction and down towards the road. The JMW actually does a detour via bridleways around Much Wenlock to Wenlock Edge, but as we are on bikes we might like to stop off in the town for refreshments first. Go left at the **B4376** for Much Wenlock, where you will arrive after a fast, easy descent of a couple of kilometres.

Wilderhope Manor

The Warden of Wilderhope Manor (and friend)

WMBR - 4

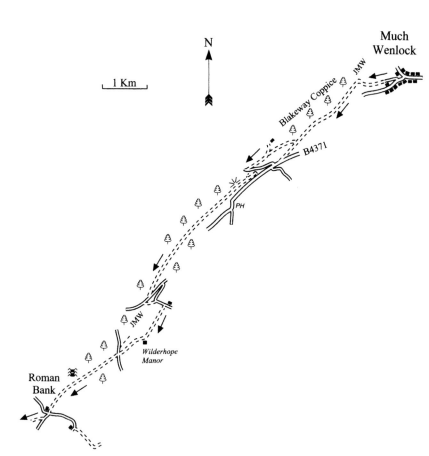

Much Wenlock to Roman Bank

Take the B4371 Church Stretton road out of Much Wenlock and after about 100m or so, go right and up Blakeway Hollow. This excellent track climbs up hill and enters some woods, Blakeway Coppice, where it rejoins the JMW. Continue on reasonably solid track, through the woodland, until eventually you arrive at a fork.

Go left at the fork, descend to a motorcycle trap and continue along a lane to a road. Cross over and climb up through woods, pass through a gate and onto a disused railway track, where you go right. After about 4km you will see a track on the left, the JMW, which climbs up through the woods to a road.

At the road, go right and down the hill a short distance, then take the excellent track left and back up into the woods (easier than the JMW, which is a muddy climb). Exit, via a steep little climb. Ignoring the JMW, which goes right, continue straight on down the lane. The track bears right, eventually passing behind **Wilderhope Manor**, and continues down the drive to a lane.

Cross over the lane, through a gate (rejoin the JMW) and follow along the right-hand edge of a field. The bridleway enters Coats Wood and after about 2km of difficult riding (?) brings you to the road junction at Roman Bank.

Long Mynd – climbing the Portway

Clun Castle

WMBR - 5

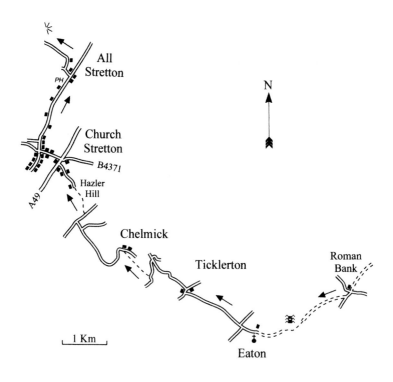

All Stretton

PH

Church Stretton

B4371

A49

Hazler Hill

Chelmick

Ticklerton

Roman Bank

Eaton

N

1 Km

Roman Bank to All Stretton

Continue straight on at the Roman Bank junction, bearing right after about 100m, through a gate and up a track. Pass a couple of cottages and climb gently on a firm rocky track. Continue on along the top of the Edge, through trees (can be soft) to arrive at a gate. Follow along the top left-hand edge of a field, then right and down the hill to another gate. Bear slightly left, up to a gate and continue up and along a tree-lined track. Enjoy a fun descent through woods on excellent track, eventually arriving at the hamlet of **Eaton**.

Follow the lane up hill for **Ticklerton** and take a right, then left, for Soudley. Just before the village, turn sharp left and back along a narrow lane. After about 400m go right where there is a JMW sign.

After going through a gate, climb steadily up a tree-lined track, which then descends through woods (can be soft) towards a stream. Continue alongside the stream on a track that improves, past cottages and into the hamlet of **Chelmick**. Go left and climb out of Chelmick, passing a farm, up towards Hazler Hill and a T-junction, where you go right.

Just before a quarry, go left and along a narrow bridleway down to a gate. Continue down (steep) through woods, cross over a stream, and through another gate, with grand views ahead of Church Stretton and Carding Mill Valley. Cross open ground, bearing slightly right, to a farm. Continue down a track, past houses to eventually arrive at a road. Go left to the main **A49**(T), and left into Church Stretton.

The JMW actually climbs up onto the Long Mynd via the Carding Mill Valley. This can be very busy and the WMBR therefore opts for a quieter route. From the centre of **Church Stretton**, head north along the B4370 towards All Stretton. At the village, go left and up Castle Hill.

WMBR - 6

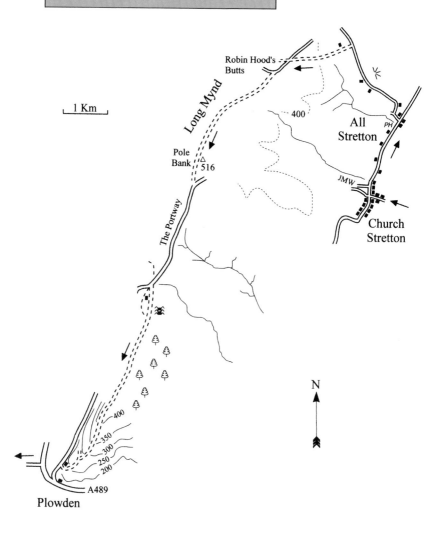

1 Km

Robin Hood's Butts

Long Mynd

400

All Stretton

PH

Pole Bank
516

JMW

The Portway

Church Stretton

N

400
350
300
250
200

A489

Plowden

All Stretton to Plowden

Climb the steep lane up to the top of Plush Hill, continuing until you arrive at a junction just before a cattle grid. Go left, up a wide gravel track, which is a bridleway, along the edge of open moorland. Eventually you come to a county road.

Go left, along the road for about 300m, then left and along a track (The Portway) in a south-westerly direction to rejoin the JMW. Cross over a road and climb up to the trig point at the summit of the Long Mynd, **Pole Bank**. After admiring the view continue on in a southerly direction to join the road. Follow the road until you arrive at the entrance to the Midland Gliding club.

The bridleway, and **The Portway**, actually follow the drive and cross the airfield. As this can be a little dangerous, take the permissive track around the western side of the airfield, the Starboardway and rejoin the bridleway to the south. Follow the grassy track, with heather and bracken on either side, past woods and along the broad top of the Mynd. This is a superb vantage point, with fine views to the west into Wales.

Descend for about a kilometre, through a gate on the left, down to another gate, across a field, and through further gates by some farm buildings. Follow the track round to the right and down to the lane. Go left here, and down to the **A489** at Plowden

WMBR - 7

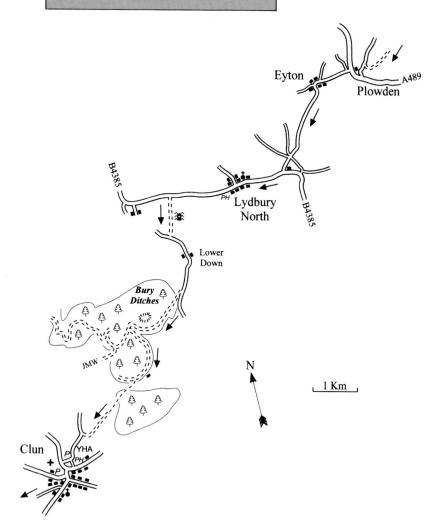

Plowden to Clun

This next section requires a bit of road work, but at least it's an opportunity to get up a bit of speed! At Plowden take the A489 west and after a few hundred metres, go left for **Eyton** and Lydbury North. Follow the road up into the village, then round to the left for Lydbury. Continue straight on at the crossroads at Five Turnings, and then right (straight on) onto the B4385.

Go through **Lydbury North** (past the Powis Arms?) and, after about 1.5km, you will see a by-way on the left. Follow this by-way, which can be soft (or even flooded!) in the wet, over the River Kemp via a couple of bridges, and up to a lane, where you go left.

The climb eases off at **Lower Down**, then continues on up more steeply. Eventually you arrive at the Forestry Commission **Bury Ditches** carpark. This is a pleasant spot to have a picnic, but an even better one is just a bit further on. Follow the JMW along the easy forestry road around the edge of Sunnyhill, with particularly splendid views to the south, looking down to Clunton.

Eventually you will see a forestry track on the left, which descends around the southern edge of Steepleknoll woods (the JMW continues straight on). This next bit is tricky, and is easily missed. Look out for a track that doubles back left to an old gate, just at the lowest point on the forestry track. Go through the gate and down onto a farm track, where there is a bridleway post. Follow the bridleway across a stream and bear right and up to a large gate by the woods. Continue along the edge of the woods, entering the woods by a further gate.

Climb up steeply into Radnor Wood (get off and push!) and then exit via a gate. Continue straight on down the right-hand side of a couple of fields on a good track. Eventually you arrive at a gate and enter a tree-lined sunken lane. Enjoy a swift descent on an excellent track, which bears right and out onto a lane, to rejoin the JMW. Go left here and down past the YHA and into Clun.

WMBR - 8

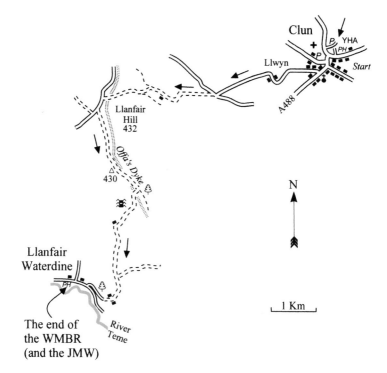

Clun

Llwyn

Start

A488

Llanfair
Hill
432

Offa's Dyke

430

N

Llanfair
Waterdine

The end of
the WMBR
(and the JMW)

River
Teme

1 Km

Clun to Llanfair Waterdine

Follow the A488 south out of Clun, past the church and then right for Springhill. The road climbs steadily up past Llwyn and eventually arrives at a crossroads.

Go right here, then immediately left where there is a bridleway sign. Follow the tarmac farm track to the farm, around the back of some barns, then on along a gravel track. In a field, bear left by an oak tree with a JMW sign and climb up to a gate at the top of the field. Continue up a shallow valley, finally arriving at a lane, where you go left and up the hill.

At the top of the hill go left along a by-way and onto a gravel track, which follows along the western side of the **Offa's Dyke**. Enjoy splendid views to the east and west, cross over the dyke, pass some barns and turn right by some conifers.

Go through a gate, over the dyke again, and then descend steeply on a rocky track. The track bears left at some barns, then descends gently, through a farm and finally through woods and down to the narrow lane at Llanfair Waterdine. Enjoy a well-earned drink at the pub, you have just completed the West Midlands Bike Route!

Appendix

Here are a few useful addresses.

COUNTY COUNCILS

Warwickshire County Council, PO Box 43, Shire Hall, Warwick, CV34 4SX.

Shropshire County Council, Shirehall, Abbey Foregate, Shrewsbury, SY2 6ND.

Worcestershire County Council, County Hall, Spetchley Road, Worcester, WR5 2NP.

Hereford Council, Engineering Services, PO Box 234, Hereford, HR1 2ZD.

Gloucestershire County Council, Shire Hall, Gloucester, GL1 2TH.

Staffordshire County Council, Green Hall, Lichfield Road, Stafford, ST17 4LA.

FORESTRY COMMISSION
Marches Forest District, Whitcliffe, Ludlow, Shropshire, SY8 2HD.

BRITISH WATERWAYS
Marketing and Communications, Willow Grange, Church Road, Watford. WD1 3QA.

CYCLISTS TOURING CLUB
Cotterell House, 69 Meadrow, Godalming, Surrey, GU7 3HS.

FOR MORE INFORMATION ABOUT OUR RANGE OF MBGs, SEE OUR WEB SITE AT **www.ernest-press.co.uk**